"Emily Wierenga is one of those rare and extraordinary writers willing to lay it all out there, every painful, private, unbecoming detail of her life. Yet somehow her story becomes your story. Yes, the details might be different but the struggles, doubts, pressures, and fears are the same. But here's where Emily rises above even the most extraordinary writers: her hopes become your hopes. Her faith becomes your faith. Her prayer becomes your prayer. Her ever-faithful God becomes your God, and through the pages of this book, you feel him pull you to his chest and assure you he has never left your side. *Making It Home* is nourishment for the heart, clarity for the eyes, and divine comfort for the soul."

Rachel Macy Stafford, *New York Times* bestselling author
of *Hands Free Mama*

"Emily gently reminds us that a home is far more than a house. When we open our doors and hearts to others—both far and near—we create a precious space where God and humanity reside richly together."

Margaret Feinberg, author of *Fight Back with Joy*

"*Making It Home* absolutely captivated me. Emily Wierenga is a brilliant writer who shares her journey with refreshing vulnerability. Her prose is poetic and raw, and the door to her spiritual life is held wide open for the reader. This book is like having ringside seats to one woman's wrestling match with God as she fights to figure out who she really is. Yes, this is Emily's story, and this is her wrestling match. But really, it's all of our stories. Reading Emily's journey, I discovered more of wh͟͟ ͟͟ ͟ ͟ ͟ ͟ ͟ ͟ ͟ ͟ ͟ ͟ ͟ more about what it means to finc͟ last, you wholly surrender." J͟

Jenn

"Emily Wierenga has a gift for taking readers on journeys of the soul. If you need hope for the future, courage for the next step, and an insightful, honest guide to walk with you, *Making It Home* will help you find your way."

Holley Gerth, *Wall Street Journal* bestselling author
of *You're Already Amazing*

"In her beautiful new memoir, *Making It Home*, Emily Wierenga writes with captivating and uncommon vulnerability, sharing the insecurities and fears that held her hostage and the dwelling place of hope she found when she was willing to courageously love and be loved, right where she was."

Renee Swope, bestselling author of *A Confident Heart*

"Emily Wierenga writes like a novelist, but the stories are her own. And somehow they are more life-giving and truth-telling than the ones people make up. But that's what happens with great stories, I suppose. They're given to those who can tell them best."

Ben Arment, author of *Dream Year* and founder of STORY

"*Making It Home* is a poignant, daringly open memoir about one girl's stretch toward love and acceptance. You will unmask yourself in Emily's journey, the final denouement being the discovery that you are utterly loved and cherished and affirmed by Jesus. A delightful, important read."

Mary DeMuth, coauthor of *The Day I Met Jesus*

"I'm glad the world has people like Emily Wierenga, people who are sincere in their weakness and can tell a story that folds a reader into it. I tend to see the world as a web of ideas. Emily, through her own struggles and God's deep grace, sees the world as a web of relationships. Most importantly, she sees God's hand in all these relationships. *Making It Home* is moving and deeply personal in an inviting and earnest way. It is hope-filled and splendidly crafted."

Barnabas Piper, author of *The Pastor's Kid* and cohost
of *The Happy Rant Podcast*

"Emily Wierenga's writing is a masterful symphony of words. In *Making It Home*, she pulls back the curtain of her heart and invites us to peek in the window at the gut-wrenching struggles and daily stresses that led her to the place where broken souls are mended and love changes everything—home."

Sharon Jaynes, author of *The Power of a Woman's Words* and *Praying for Your Husband from Head-to-Toe*

"Poignant. Gritty. Beautiful. This is one woman's search to find the ever-present love of her heavenly Father amidst diapers and crayons, cancers and eating disorders, miscarriages and broken hearts. I felt as though she peeked into my soul and filled the emptiness with truth. Don't miss it."

Susan May Warren, award-winning, bestselling author of *The Wonder of You*

"Reminiscent of Anne Lamott and Ann Voskamp, Emily Wierenga has written a new book that is a mix of poetic story, real-life struggles, and penetrating truth. *Making It Home* is one woman's journey of discovering that *who she is* means more than *what she does*, especially within the four walls of her home. Emily's story is my story. It's the story of every woman who allows God to peel back the layers of self-protection to discover the beauty that he sees within us and the joy in the family and home he's made for us. Highly recommended!"

Tricia Goyer, *USA Today* bestselling author of fifty books, including *Teen Mom: You Are Stronger Than You Think*

"Rich and raw, Emily shares about *Making It Home*—a place where you can fall, rage, and eventually even heal. An authentic picture of messy but beautiful grace."

Sheila Wray Gregoire, marriage blogger at ToLoveHonorandVacuum.com

"Emily is mastering the art of finding God in the everyday moments of life. Her writing will help you do the same. A beautiful read."

Brooke McGlothlin, cofounder and president of Raising Boys Ministries and coauthor of *Hope for the Weary Mom: Let God Meet You in the Mess*

"*Making It Home* is a story of the heart. In this book, Emily not only shares the steps of her own journey but invites you along as well."

Claire Diaz-Ortiz, Silicon Valley innovator, early Twitter employee, and author

making it home

Other Books by Emily T. Wierenga

Atlas Girl: Finding Home in the Last Place I Thought to Look

A Promise in Pieces

*Mom in the Mirror: Body Image, Beauty, and Life after Pregnancy
(cowritten with Dena Cabrera)*

*Chasing Silhouettes: How to Help a Loved One
Battling an Eating Disorder*

making it home

Finding My Way to Peace, Identity, and Purpose

EMILY T. WIERENGA

BakerBooks

a division of Baker Publishing Group
Grand Rapids, Michigan

Published by Baker Books
a division of Baker Publishing Group
P.O. Box 6287, Grand Rapids, MI 49516-6287
www.bakerbooks.com

Printed in the United States of America

Library of Congress Cataloging-in-Publication Data
Wierenga, Emily T., 1980–
    Making it home : finding my way to peace, identity, and purpose / Emily T. Wierenga.
        pages cm
    ISBN 978-0-8010-1695-0 (pbk.)
    1. Wierenga, Emily T., 1980– 2. Christian biography—Canada. 3. Christian women—Religious life. I. Title.
BR1725.W4485A3 2015
270.8′3092—dc23   2015007055
[B]

Published in association with MacGregor Literary Agency.

15   16   17   18   19   20   21   7   6   5   4   3   2   1

In keeping with biblical principles of creation stewardship, Baker Publishing Group advocates the responsible use of our natural resources. As a member of the Green Press Initiative, our company uses recycled paper when possible. The text paper of this book is composed in part of post-consumer waste.

Dedicated to my friend Ashley—for having the humility to admit you were lost, and the courage to make it home.

Your people will rebuild the ancient ruins
    and will raise up the age-old foundations;
you will be called Repairer of Broken Walls,
    Restorer of Streets with Dwellings.

                                        Isaiah 58:12

We shall not cease from exploration
And the end of all our exploring
Will be to arrive where we started
And know the place for the first time.

                                        T. S. Eliot

Contents

11

PART 3 • MOTHER

PART 4 • WOMAN

PART 5 • DAUGHTER

PART I

Child

I believe in pink. I believe that laughing is the best calorie burner. I believe in kissing, kissing a lot. I believe in being strong when everything seems to be going wrong. I believe that happy girls are the prettiest girls. I believe that tomorrow is another day and I believe in miracles.

Audrey Hepburn

Homeless

How often have I lain beneath rain on a strange roof, thinking of home.

William Faulkner

September 2013

"One more song," he says, pulling me close in the afternoon light.

It's Sunday and the boys are napping. Trent smells like wood smoke and I've still got my church clothes on.

One more song. It's what he used to say when we were eighteen and lying on the carpet in my townhouse at midnight, and now we're thirty-three and lying in bed in the middle of the day, and yet it feels the same—this place where I can feel his heartbeat. It's my home.

The slowing of his breath, now, and he's asleep.

The house is so silent on the Sabbath, except for the third from the bottom stair, which creaks when I step on it, and I pause, hoping the kids won't wake.

Continue past the entrance with its piles of boots and shoes and jackets, up the second set of stairs into the open space of hardwood and long counters and wide windows, JOY across the top of the stove in red stencils from Michael's. The counter has crumbs on it, the air smells like tomato soup and grilled cheese.

I make apple cinnamon tea in a mug I bought off the street in Korea, sit down in the living room easy chair. The tan one, across from the window looking out at the hamlet of Neerlandia. Three deer, now, peering at me from across the road, their white tails flashing like the tips of swords in the sun, and they're ducking into the woods. Our town of one hundred, quietly nestled amid farms and a crescent of elderly and young families, the co-op at one end and three churches at the other.

I can't rest for remembering her.

The woman in the old man's jacket.

I found her one week ago in Edmonton, two hours from here. I was on my way to visit a friend in the hospital and I'd stopped at a Wendy's to use the bathroom. I walked in behind a mother and her daughter and we all stopped because there were two skinny legs in men's pants, with white socks and black slippers sticking out from beneath a stall door. I thought it was a man, and I thought he was dead.

But it was a woman and she was stumbling but alive, rising and apologizing, and she had rich brown skin, coarse hair cropped close, and the reddest eyes. She wore an old man's winter coat, the hood pulled low, and she exited slowly from the bathroom but she didn't smell like she'd been drinking. Or like anything, really, except the dankness of an unwashed body.

There was an empty pop can in the stall. She'd spent the night there.

I followed her from the bathroom, until she turned around and saw me. "Can I buy you lunch?" I asked, and she nodded, walked up to the counter, ordered chili and a coffee, then went and laid her head down on a table. I paid for the food and brought her the tray, and she ate without chewing.

"I'm Emily," I said.

She looked up at me then, and smiled. "I'm Leah."

Her smile exploded off her face like my friend Zoe's in Congo when I was two, me staring through the fence at my neighbors, wanting to touch their night-skin, the light in their eyes.

But Leah's smile faded fast and she shook her head and looked down, as though she'd made a mistake.

I reached across the table then, touched her arm, and she flinched. I asked if she had anywhere she could go, anywhere I could drop her off, and she shook her head.

"I'm from Vancouver," she said, tattoos lining her wrists, black tribal ink. "I don't know no one here. No friends, no family. No one."

I decided, then, that she could rest in the back of my van— the second seat was pulled, the back empty. It was autumn, mid-October, but the sun was shining and the temperature around twenty degrees Celsius.

"I'm visiting someone in the hospital across the road," I said. "You can sleep until I'm done, okay?"

"Okay," she said, rising immediately, because it was better than a bathroom stall. We walked outside; I gave her my coat to use as a pillow and she curled up in the back of my Dodge, the red Caravan Uncle George had gotten us for six hundred dollars at an auction. In a moment she was snoring.

I wanted to bring her home. We have a guest room and I wanted to give her a bed and a bathroom and home-cooked meals because everyone deserves a home. A place to find themselves, a place to know they are more than a number, but when I called Trent he said she needed more help than we could give her.

So after my hospital visit, I dropped her off at the Hope Mission with its beds and its programs and its long line of men in scruffy beards, and my heart ached the two hours back to Neerlandia. It ached for the world's Leahs who have no one to make them supper, no one to care if they've gone missing, no physical address or postal box, and God showed me her room in heaven, then.

He showed me a soft, high bed with a dozen pillows and a large Jacuzzi bath and the tallest, widest windows full of sunshine. He showed me food on a buffet table, and it was all for Leah. And I know that whoever calls on Jesus's name will have a room waiting, the kind that belongs to skinny legs lying in bathroom stalls.

That night I was tucking Aiden in, and I was praying with him, my three-year-old with the long lashes and serious eyes, but I kept seeing Leah's face.

"I met a woman today," I told him. "She has no home."

He turned to me, his eyes wide. "She has no home?!" he said. "We have to help them!"

Yes, honey. We have to help them.

I'm sitting and drinking my tea from the Korean mug, the house breathing around me. I'm reading Anne Lamott's *Traveling Mercies*, but for a moment I fold the page, close the cover, lean back, and remember Korean days: that tiny square apartment beside the fire station, stamps in our passports, and as many countries as possible stitched onto my backpack.

I had studied the Lonely Planet guidebook and learned the language on tape in the months before Trent and I moved to Wonju, a city nestled in the mountains east of Seoul, and we taught English there, for a year, traveling to Japan and China and Thailand on the weekends, and now I study cookbooks. I plan homeschool, and some days, like today, I stare out the window with a mug of tea and wonder how I got here.

In this farming community north of Edmonton where moose sleep on our front lawn; where we don't need to pay for groceries because the co-op has our account number; where the post office is in the back of the grocery store and the only Christian public school in the country is just down the street, the same school my husband teaches at.

And even as our house slumbers, it's alive—with peanut-butter kisses on the windows and red wine stains on the carpet.

Home is *Uncle John's Bathroom Reader* beside the toilet, the smell of a strawberry rhubarb candle a lady from church brought me when I miscarried. I light it every time I have a shower. It smells like mercy.

Home is the pile of books, *Thomas the Train* and *Dora the Explorer* and *Winnie the Pooh*, thrown from Kasher's bed because he always pages through them before he goes to sleep and then he habitually tosses them. It's the bear's ear stuck in his mouth, which he sucks. It's the infant newness that still clings to his two-year-old cheek during sleep.

It's the long lashes of Aiden, the green bunny in his arms and the flashlight by his hand. It's his footy pajamas with the feet cut off because he's three and a half and has broken through the toes.

Beside me, a rough-hewn bookshelf made by Trent out of barn boards. There's the coffee table made from the same boards, the children's chairs—Mickey, Minnie, and Dora, which are bent out of shape from Aiden and Kasher using them to wrestle.

Home is the pile of dirty clothes by Trent's side of the bed, the stack of books on both of our bedside tables—mine all literary or devotional and his all historical or fantasy, and us meeting in the middle under a feather tick. It is the smell of baby powder fabric softener.

Home is me climbing the stairs to the kitchen, some of the crab apples we picked still piled in a bucket and the rest turning into apple leather in the oven. Bowls of apple juice waiting to be frozen on the counter, and it's Trent emerging from the office and seeing me. Saying, "It feels like I haven't seen you in forever," when really it's been twenty minutes.

It's the smell of his skin when he pulls me in, and me whispering, "Not by the kitchen window," because it's a small town—maybe one thousand people on Sundays when the farmers pile into church—and we have no curtains. So he takes me into the guest room.

The house hums like it's in love: the dryer's tenor, the dishwasher's soprano, and the refrigerator with its low bass. I walk now, to the bathroom, look at myself in the mirror, at the fine wrinkles by my eyes—I have my father's eyes.

I have his heart too, his nomadic heart that took us to Africa when I was only two.

I remember walking home from school one day feeling like someone had split my heart open like a melon. Nothing had really happened that day. I was a kid in university, and the sun was shining when I bent over from the pain—and no matter how tightly my boyfriend held me against the rough cotton of his shirt, my chest throbbed.

It wasn't anything medical and I knew this because it had happened a year earlier too, on the hill outside Mount Carmel Bible School—a grassy hill where I fell and sobbed after watching a video of Mother Teresa tending to the leprous and dying in India.

And it happened again, fifteen years later on my way home from Uganda, and my heart cracked open across the airplane bathroom and I gripped the edge of the sink like I was in labor.

"When I was a girl, I grew from five foot seven to six foot in a few months," a friend told me. "My legs would shoot with growing pains, and it's kind of how my heart feels a lot of times. Like its legs are growing—and the greater number of places I visit and the more people I meet, the more distance I put on my heart and the greater it hurts."

It's like our hearts are homeless, which feels almost crude to say, because at the time of writing this four hundred villagers in northern Uganda have lost their grass huts to wildfires and they are literally without a home.

But our hearts—they wander around outside our bodies without a place of residence.

When I was a child, I lived in a house that didn't always feel like home.

I'd moved ten times by the age of seven. To places like Nigeria and Congo, where my parents worked with the blind, and then all over Southern Ontario with its small towns dotted between fields, and Northern Ontario with its jagged rocks and thick brush.

I stopped talking when we moved to Nigeria, and even though I'd started again at age four when we moved back to Canada I never really caught up with everything I wanted to say. Like a wad of unspoken longing in my chest.

High school was spent in a split-level house near Echo Bay, Ontario, its maple trees tapped in winter for sap, whose leaves caught fire like thousands of torches every autumn—valleys of flame, every time I walked the country road.

Our house was a brick structure. I'd lie for hours on blankets, suntanning in the grass, journaling about boys. Boys filled in the blank pages, and I plastered my bedroom walls with them too, and none of them lasted very long, just long enough for them to realize I wouldn't sleep with them and then we'd break up.

I wasn't starving myself anymore—I was done with that, for a while, the hospital at age thirteen, and nurses looking in horror at this purple-skinned girl whose braces showed through her cheeks, and they said I was a miracle.

All I knew was I was cold.

I'd stopped eating at age nine because I was a lonely home-schooled minister's daughter, and one of my only friends—an elderly woman who taught me how to knit and played cards with me—had died one day without warning.

So I'd stopped eating, because there was a hole in me no food could fill.

I missed Dad, who was never home, always visiting this person or that or working on his sermon, and Mum was overrun with children—all four of us on her heels, and her feeding and clothing and schooling us on Dr. James Dobson and a shoestring budget.

I spent a lot of time in my room with the door closed. We had family meetings once a month and Dad would tell us how much we could spend on heat because he worked part-time at a little white church forty-five minutes away, and part-time as a chaplain for the army, always working. And Mum took care of her mother—my Nanny—who lived in the house next door.

There was good too, as there's light with the dark, and home was this place with a piano and the smell of bread baking and four kids, chatting. Dad would spend hours helping me with my math homework each night. He made us a playhouse in the woods and taught us recorder and piano. He wrestled with my brother on the floor and we always hoped he had time to read us a story. We liked sitting on his lap, feeling the scruff of his beard against our cheek, Mum crocheting or mending in the corner.

My tea is gone. The sun is setting fast as it does in the fall, like it can't wait to tuck behind fleecy clouds, and I hear my boys rising. Whimpering in their bunk beds, and Trent's calling them. "Aiden, Kasher, come to Daddy," and their feet on the rungs of the ladder and the carpet, running, through our bedroom door and onto the bed. And I smile, because I know I'll find them all huddled under the feather tick.

I place my mug in the sink and find my way down, past the creaky stairs, into that room, and the boys squeal when they see me and we all hold each other in the fading light of the afternoon.

And I hurt for Leah—like dozens of trapped birds flapping against my rib cage—and I wonder whether or not she is still alive. The woman with the skinny legs and the man's jacket who slept in the back of my van.

Because for all the home around me, I used to be her.

And home is making me.

2

Work

The ache for home lives in all of us. The safe place where we can go as we are and not be questioned.

Maya Angelou

August 2011

Kasher has just turned one month old.

He's a little boy in a vibrating chair at my elbow, watching me with his father's eyes, in blue overalls, and he's big for his age, his older brother napping downstairs.

I'm typing at the dining room table. My fingers smell like bananas and I've still got a half-eaten piece of toast on my plate. One of my paintings hangs on the orange wall behind me; it's big, with sunflowers, textured with acrylic paint and salt. I have paintings hung all over my house, and the dining room, kitchen, and living room are open. When I talk, my quiet voice carries to the edge of the house, touching every room, and this is important to me.

When I was young I was never asked for my opinion. I was never asked my favorite anything, and I was encouraged to be quiet and polite. I still forget I have a voice. I still prefer painting and written words. Because no one can interrupt a picture or an essay.

I haven't been paid in nine months for the articles I've been writing for a newspaper, and I only realized this last week. I just kept expecting them to send the money, and they didn't, because they're broke, and I'm done. I'm done doing interviews and spending hours writing stories I won't be paid for, and it's been years of journalism. Writing people's inspiring stories for faith publications, and my spirit is dry.

Kasher has the chubbiest cheeks. He is drooling and trying to smile; I can see it pulling on the edge of his lips as he watches his mommy write a novel, the one that will give me a name, I've decided. I've been working all my life trying to make something of myself. I was the seven-year-old who never played, who sat at her desk learning to draw cartoons and writing poetry because I wanted to make something of myself, to feel the "I love you" people said but didn't show.

I wrote a novel when Aiden was born too. I was going to take six months off, but there was so much time in our bungalow with the overarching trees and the bedrooms with no closets. Aiden would jump in his jolly jumper, a bib around his neck, and I'd sit with my laptop and my words. Trying to say what I never could to Mum: Why don't you smile? And to Dad: Why don't you want to stay home and play with me?

I only write when Aiden's sleeping now. I don't want to be the mother that doesn't play, so I read lots of stories and I chase him around the island and we do homeschool, learning shapes and colors, but Kasher's so small I still write when he's awake, and I dread the day when Aiden stops napping.

Because who will I be then?

When the words stop my voice stops too. The voice of the little girl, the one who was taught to be seen and not heard, and I'm fighting for her now. I'm fighting to be heard.

Kasher's cooing and the clock is ticking. I'm writing a love story about a boy who loves a girl, and it's my story. Trent loves this broken girl and I want to prove to him, somehow, that I'm not just a mother, as though that's something he wants me to be; that I'm not just an unwashed head of hair or a shirt with spit-up, that I'm not just a pile of coupons on the counter or a bowlful of dough, rising, but something literary that will last.

And Trent holds me at night as I cry because the words are never enough, and he tells me I am more. "You are amazing," he says. "Remember how you said you would be happy once you published a book? Well, you've got one." I do. A book no one has heard of, because it was commissioned by a now-nonexistent ministry.

"And you've got all of those articles—and you're a wonderful mom." And he goes on, his voice in my hair, but it doesn't matter what anyone says to me, because there aren't accomplishments enough to affirm the three-year-old inside who still can't talk, the nine-year-old who decided to stop eating, the sixteen-year-old who was dumped for being too nice.

Kasher's starting to fuss, and I save my document, my 49,000 words, and I take my youngest to the couch to nurse him, the afternoon light falling on our hair and his cheek soft against my chest. I love to watch his hands weave and then tuck, and sometimes he folds them in a prayer but mostly he drinks like he can't get enough, his whole body arching and stretching and then relaxing.

This is when I rest. Holding him, it's like a Sabbath for this girl who began offering homemade cards for sale in local shops when she was fourteen. None of the cards sold, and at fifteen I was taking Watkins and Regal products door-to-door after school. We were given forty dollars a month to buy everything from clothes to deodorant, so I learned early to save a dollar. But I also learned early to work hard so I could afford the kinds of clothes my mother never could. Clothes from brands like Northern Reflections and

Roots and Bluenotes. And I wondered if it was possible for Christians to be successful.

Kasher's wearing secondhand overalls and our toys are all from the thrift store but the couch I'm sitting on is new, and this somehow makes me feel better about myself, like I've done something right. And maybe if I sell my novel and it becomes a bestseller we won't ever have to worry about money again.

Flashback, now, to us kids crowded on the couch, Dad at the easel with a marker talking to us about the budget and where we can spend money and how we can save.

I would have a warm house, I decided. I would have cereal in the cupboard—not just homemade granola—and I would use Bounce in the dryer because our towels were always stiff from the clothesline, and I would buy my kids shampoo and deodorant. And we'd eat out every Sunday after church.

Kasher's done now; he's all warm and full and I'm burping him against my shoulder. The sun makes a pool at our feet and I wish I could just hold him. I wish I could just rock him and sing to him. I wish I could take a nap. I wish I could paint my nails or bake for a whole afternoon or slowly hang laundry on the line.

But I don't let myself do any of those things because I have to write two thousand words a day or I won't feel complete. There's an urgency in my chest like a congregation of women beating rugs.

"Mama . . ."

Aiden's calling me from downstairs and naptime is over. I've only written five hundred words today and I'm tired. I don't want to mess this mother thing up but I want to be known beyond these four walls because the world tells me I need to be more.

The world tells me I should be pumping my breast milk and doing office work and that I can wear a business suit and have a nanny and that motherhood is not enough because it's unseen and unpaid and traditional.

Mum tells me that's not true but she was never happy when we were young, and maybe if I can write enough words and get published enough and sell enough books then maybe, one day, Dad will look up from his keyboard and see the little girl in her nightgown standing at his elbow.

Aiden's peering up at me from his bed, his cheeks flushed from sleep, and I carefully pick him up; I balance both boys on my hips and carry them to the blue chair in the den. The giant chalkboard on the wall is covered in ABCs and 123s and I hold them, smell their hair, tell them how much I love them.

I hear the garage door open and Trent's home; he bikes each day to the Christian public school down the road where he's a junior high teacher and his footsteps, now, echo across the deck strewn with bikes and leaves and lined with flowers.

"Daddy's home," I say in a whisper and Aiden explodes off my lap, to head for the door, just as it opens, and he clamors up the stairs.

Trent comes down holding Aiden by his feet and Aiden's laughing. Trent leans in and kisses me. "How was your day?" he says. He smells like the wind, his eyes are bright, and he's tall with a dark goatee. My heart still hurts sometimes when I look at him, because he's a good man who folds laundry for me and dances to make me laugh.

We're a family when Trent's here, his school bag hanging on the peg by the door, and he's always the first to leave work because he misses his boys.

It's time to pull out meat and start supper. I'm making tacos.

But even as the beef fries and I listen to the sounds of the boys downstairs I'm thinking of my characters, the arc of my story, and supper burns even as I try to find the words.

The ones that will save me.

"I don't know how to tell you this, Emily, but—they said no." I'm on the phone with my agent two weeks after giving birth to my nearly nine-pound Kasher.

"It's been so long," I whisper. It's all the breath left in me.

"I know—I'm so sorry," she says, and we're silent together, except for my hiccupping sobs. An editor has been courting my manuscript for a year, and after three hundred and sixty-five days of waiting, the publishing board has said no and I have nothing.

Forgetting how doctors had said I wouldn't be able to have children, forgetting about the miracle that lies in my arms and the other one that's coloring a picture at the Ikea kids' table. Forgetting about the man who lives to make me laugh, who's making wine in the kitchen, forgetting the sound of Mum's voice on the end of the line, the voice of a woman I'd feared would die but who now lives healed of her brain tumor.

Forgetting that a book deal is not what gives me a name, but it's all I hear: the sound of rejection on the other end of the line, the sound of me, being made a fool, for all my waiting and hoping. The champagne bottle unopened in the fridge.

"Everything okay?" Trent mouths the words at me. I shake my head. Kasher asleep in my arms and my agent telling me I should spend some time writing what I want to write. To put this book aside and just do something that brings me joy.

I don't know what that means. I don't know how to do anything for joy. And then I remember dating Trent. I remember that kiss in the rain outside his townhouse; I remember hours on the carpet with my head on his chest, talking, listening to the radio; I remember midnight bike rides to Rundle Park, playing Frisbee golf, and watching movies just to hold each other's hand.

A joy that writes what it wants to.

"All right," I say, and my agent prays with me and we say goodbye.

I wonder how long she will put up with me. I haven't sold anything yet and Aiden's showing me his picture. It's a scribble of green marker—his favorite color—and he's got green on his lips and he's smiling but his eyebrows are raised. He's wondering if I like it, and he's only two. His mommy's fears course through him and I kneel down and hug him, tell him, "It's magnificent, son, I can't wait to hang it on the fridge," and his small body relaxes.

He knows in this moment that I love him because I said I like his picture, but I want for him what I want for me: a long-lasting sense of self in spite of what the world tells him. I want him to be so at peace that he can sleep in the boat while the storm rocks and I want him to know without a shadow of a doubt the confidence that makes a person walk on water.

And maybe if I learn it, he will too.

I begin that night to outline my novel and I've given up on the eating disorder book. Publishers say it's niche and I'm an unknown author. So I begin to write about dating Trent, about the things that bring me joy.

And one year later, I'll be sitting at a table at a conference for American Christian Counselors and a box will arrive. I'll be shaking as I open it, my friend standing there—and I'll look up at him and he'll smile. "It's like Christmas, isn't it?" he'll say, this author of twentysome books.

And I'll take it out—my eating disorder manuscript that has finally been published by a small family publisher willing to take a chance—and I'll hold it close, as though it's a promise.

It will be the first time I've seen my book, released a week earlier, and I'll be flipping through the crisp white pages when my eyes catch a glitch—fifty pages missing from the middle of the book. I'll keep flipping and find them, those missing pages, bunched together at the end. I'll look through the box and every single copy is exactly the same—with the middle section missing like someone's taken a bite out of my dream.

Counselors, hundreds of them, everywhere, walking by oblivious and I'll be clutching at my heart because for a moment I'd felt full.

My friend will look at me, even as I'm wiping at my eyes. "What's wrong?" he'll say. I'll show him the missing pages and he'll assure me that the publisher will fix it, say we need to get ahold of them right away.

"God is always trying to humble me," I'll say, putting the books back in the box.

But what I don't know then is that God is *for* me. He is for me in spite of these disappointments, in spite of three years of waiting for a contract, plus one year of an editor courting it only to reject it, and then this. He is for me in spite of what anyone else says or thinks because he is my Father, and the Bible says he sings over me. He delights in me. He died for me. No matter the number of pages missing.

That night I will lie awake for a long time in my hotel bed—the sky like long streaks of black permanent marker through the blinds.

My prayer had been answered—yet it wasn't enough. It would never be enough. Because what I needed could not be found inside a box.

3

Little Spaces

I am content to fill a little space if God be glorified.

Susannah Wesley

September 2011

I think of her when I'm stooped on the bathroom tile cleaning up the pee from Aiden's failed attempt to empty the potty by himself, and he's on my back pretending I'm a horse, yelling, "Giddyup, Mama!"

I think of her when I let him finger paint at the kitchen table right after I've cleaned the house and soon I'm scrubbing paint off chairs and walls and even painted footprints across the hardwood.

I think of her when I find Aiden covered face to foot in my hand lotion, or sticky from eating the whole box of Vicks cough drops. When nine loads of laundry sit atop the dryer and I'm unable to get off the couch to fold them. When my son falls down the stairs or I burn supper or I step outside onto the back deck where the trees stand tall, where we watch the thunderstorms, where the birds nest and hatch, and I breathe.

I think of Susannah Wesley, mother of many, who lost seven of her nineteen children. She was the youngest of twenty-five, her father a clergyman and she married a pastor, and I wonder how she did it. How did she homeschool twelve shining faces around the kitchen table while stoking the fire while making wax candles while mending her husband's socks? How did she not only raise intelligent children but sons and daughters who feared God more than man?

I still remember sitting around my kitchen table, the eldest of four, and Mum teaching us to put "i before e," and do our multiplication tables, and always a Scripture lesson. Our house full of library books and books on tape, and when Dad was home he'd teach us French or piano. Once a month we were taught about a country, what they wore, how they spoke, what they believed, and at night we'd eat their traditional cuisine, and I still remember groundnut stew, a Nigerian dish of peanut butter sauce and beef over rice. We ate it on the floor, on a blanket woven by a blind lady from the Congo. I remember that stew because it was around then I began dieting, but I couldn't stop eating the peanut sauce, the chunks of beef on rice. And I spent the whole night wishing I hadn't because now I couldn't eat breakfast or lunch the next day and I'd have to skip rope for an hour to wear off the calories.

And I know Susannah's husband, Samuel, was difficult when he was home, idealistic and argumentative, but she was stubborn too. Once when Samuel was praying for King William, whom Susannah didn't support, she refused to say Amen, and Samuel left home that night, saying, "If we have two kings, we must have two beds."[1]

Eventually they reconciled and out of that reconciliation was born their son John, who changed the course of church history by founding the Methodist movement.

1. Anne Adams, "Susannah Wesley: Mother of Methodism," *History's Women*, accessed February 17, 2015, http://historyswomen.com/womenoffaith /SusannahWesley.html.

This gives me great hope. This conceiving a God-fearing son from the remnants of a fight.

Because I'm as stubborn as an old Dodge in the middle of winter.

There was one week when Trent gave me three candles.

The trees prematurely balding with their hair flung colorfast on asphalt, the clouds frozen to blue, and the birds flocking in dozens past our house in perfect Vs, their honking enough to wake winter.

Inside, soup, potato-creamy, orange with carrot and dill-green, soft on baby's tongue, and I am scooping in a hurry but not fast enough to feed the hunger and we are home from church, and I don't know how to stop.

This speaking in haste, this halting prayer-thoughts and turning on anger-voice, this dividing of self after a sermon on unity.

And there is a falling in my spirit, a shedding of color, and the streets are bare and the winter is chill within.

One minute I live in peace, kissing my husband's cheek and loving on my children, and the next I'm a two-year-old begging attention, crying stupid.

He hands me a candle.

It is the third one.

It has been a week of candles. First, at night after coming home late, having visited a girl hospitalized for cutting, my heart weeping, and the dishes not done and I am silent but stone and he slips out the front door and reappears with a white candle. It smells like sugar cookies.

Two evenings later, he slips out again after snow-cold blow-over and I don't know where he's gone but moments later a second candle: this time, apple.

"I thought it might smell nice," he says shyly.

And Sunday, a third candle. Cinnamon.

Because he doesn't know how to say he's sorry for all the pain. Trent's not a talker, he's a giver, and he gives hugs, he gives time, he gives candles.

And this is the key: to light the marriage-match and keep it burning. Because otherwise, the candle grows cold.

And we find each other over the flame, this boy and girl who used to kiss in the rain, and I'm thawing.

I fear for my children in those moments. Because sometimes Trent hurts my feelings or I don't show him respect and I cry or he gets frustrated and I know they're seeing it all. And we always make sure to hug and work it out in front of them too, and I often bend on one knee and look them in the eyes and say, "It's okay, honey. Mommy and Daddy still love each other."

Because home needs to be a safe place. A place to fall.

Timothy Keller says there is no such thing as hurt feelings. Only a hurt ego. "Have you ever thought about the fact that you do not notice your body until there is something wrong with it?" He writes,

> When we are walking around, we are not usually thinking how fantastic our toes are feeling. . . . That is because the parts of our body only draw attention to themselves if there is something wrong with them. The ego often hurts. That is because it has something incredibly wrong with it. Something unbelievably wrong with it. . . . There is something wrong with my sense of self. It is never happy. It is always drawing attention to itself.[2]

I'm trying to let my wounded ego lead me to Jesus.

Susannah needed Jesus early every morning before her dozen awoke; they found her on her knees and I've tried that. I tried rising before the sun and making a mug of coffee and reading Scripture and praying because I remember my Dad and Mum bowing in prayer for their kids, but I kept falling asleep.

So I do my devotions at the breakfast table instead while the kids watch a show because that's the only way I get them done, and still my insides hurt. And so many Christian books talk about joy.

2. Timothy Keller, *The Freedom of Self-Forgetfulness: The Path to True Christian Joy* (Chorley, England: 10Publishing, 2012), 16–17.

Yesterday Kasher cried nonstop in his swing. He's one of those babies who cries for hours and I tried everything until I wanted to run away and that's when I tucked him into his swing and turned, discovered Aiden had broken a DVD. He'd just snapped it in two and he was holding both pieces in his chubby hands looking down at the carpet, and I yelled at him. He started sobbing in the living room and Kasher was angry in the swing and I was crying in the office, staring out the window at the blue sky, the same sky that helped me when I was pushing my babies out, the sky I looked to for refuge in between contractions. I looked to it then and suddenly I heard it.

Footsteps, running back and forth, back and forth, and I poked my head out of the office door and found Aiden, running back and forth to the swing bringing desperate attempts to soothe his brother's crying and Kasher, piled high with blankets and toys.

It was an act of utter selflessness. Oh, to be like a child. Here I was, wanting someone to mother me, and Aiden had taken it upon himself to mother Kasher.

Every day, we as mothers put ourselves last for our families, until one day we snap because we're feeling so loveless.

I am learning. To buy an outfit for myself. To turn on the TV for the boys so I can do my devotions, but there's still a pit inside me, a bottomless pit where a little girl cries.

I read somewhere that over twenty thousand mothers in the United States alone suffer from severe depression. I wonder if this is because we feel the need to be more than we are. More than "just" a mother. Susannah found grace in being small, in doing small things, in serving small people so they might know a great God. She knew who she was.

Who am I?

I'm born to a reverend and a homeschooling mum. I'm granddaughter to agnostic British grandparents who painted canvases together and struggled with sadness and ended up divorcing; I'm granddaughter to a Scottish grandmother who loved God and battled anxiety and a Scottish grandfather who tilled fields and fought in World War II. I'm wife to a man who chops his own firewood and molds the minds of junior high students and I'm mother to two soft-spoken boys.

But who am I?

The girl with dreadlocks and three tattoos who hates ironing, refuses to wear high heels, and cries when drivers flip her the finger.

That girl. The one who keeps pulling on my clothes in the morning and wearing my deodorant.

Who is she?

4

The Dinner Table

After a good dinner one can forgive anybody, even one's own relations.

Oscar Wilde

October 2011

The air smells of fermented plums. The ground is purple, littered with fruit, and the leaves on the willows a mottled orange.

It is Thanksgiving Sunday in Canada, and we've been to church and our clothes are wrinkled, the boys in the backseat of the Subaru. I keep frowning at myself in the side mirror. We are driving to a family gathering in Westlock, forty minutes away, but all I want is a novel and a cup of tea.

A couple of weeks ago we had family photos taken with Trent's parents, Marge and Harvey, and his sisters, Teshah and Teneale and their spouses and kids and all of us stretched long beside the barn—and I hadn't recognized myself.

Kasher born three months earlier but my body, still giving birth. My breasts tender and swollen and my skin marked with zigzags across my stomach. My thighs thick and my face round and Trent says I am beautiful. He loves my curves.

"I don't want you to change—I think you're perfect," he says at night when I force myself to get naked in front of him.

Yet I'm finding it hard to eat again.

Maybe because of the photos.

But maybe too because of the news Trent's parents gave us later that day, after the photographer had gone home.

We were sitting in their living room—all blue and clean with its vacuumed rugs and wildlife paintings—Aiden playing with his cousins and Kasher in my arms and Harvey sitting on the couch, Marge twisting her hands like a dishcloth.

"Your mother has some news to tell you," Harvey began, his voice gruff, "and it's difficult for her to say so I'm going to do it for her. She went to the doctor's the other day for a mammogram," and here my breath caught, "and they found a lump."

Trent's youngest sister, Teshah, began sobbing beside Marge, and Teneale wiped her eyes.

Harvey cleared his throat. "They did a biopsy and it was malignant. She has cancer."

Everything in my head became very quiet while the girls clung to Marge. Trent sat very still.

Both he and I were still reeling from my own Mum's cancer, from three years of feeding her and bathing her and clothing her and clipping her toenails. She was recovering now, but cancer had found another mother.

It was so quiet, I said something foolish like, "I read a statistic the other day that says that one out of eight women gets breast cancer," and Teshah glared at me. I didn't blame her.

"Why would you say that?" she said, and I stammered, "But the good news is, most of them recover," and I wished I would stop talking.

Trent asked about chemo, and Marge said, "I don't know anything yet. I have an appointment with a surgeon coming up, then surgery in November, and we will find out more."

She looked at us, and she looked strong. She didn't look like she had cancer. Her hair so full and brown, and in a few months she'd be wearing a wig. "I know this is hard news, but we are in God's hands and we need to trust him. The Lord is my shepherd, and we shall not want. We need to decide now to trust God with this, no matter what happens."

Trent said he would pray and we all bowed our heads in the living room, the grandkids playing trains, the smell of pizza in the oven.

The parking lot in Westlock is full of cars. The entrance to the building is piled with shoes—mostly crocs and a couple pairs of cowboy boots, and I smell turkey and stuffing.

"Hello, hello!" Auntie Jean pulls us close and the room swarms with relatives, aunts and uncles and cousins, a pool table that Harvey leans over, cue in hand, and a counter piled with Grandma Neumann's pierogies, garden potatoes with dill, roasted ham and turkey, stuffing, three kinds of salads, and flaky white buns.

"Remember—the buns go in your pocket so you have more room on your plate," Trent whispers, and my smile is a pencil line. There will be pie too, but I am tired of the elastic on my pants. I am tired of feeling pregnant, and I am tired of cancer.

Marge is in an apron and she's smiling, running up to us. "Boys, it's so good to see you!" She pulls Aiden and Kasher close, kissing their cheeks like she hadn't just seen them yesterday. Like she isn't sick.

Two days after Kasher was born, Trent had picked me up from the hospital and driven me to Marge's. She'd led me to the couch, had told me to lie down—had brought me an egg salad sandwich on homemade bread, a cup of coffee, and we'd watched cooking shows all afternoon.

I refuse the piece of key lime pie and the stuffing that day in Westlock; I eat some turkey breast and some cooked carrots and then I glance down at Kasher who is nursing, feeding off my food, and I swallow hard.

For not knowing how to eat after all these years. For not knowing what to do with all the pain.

Dad would sit at one end of the long, scratched wooden table with the Bible, and Mum beside him. She'd dish up our meals but I'd long stopped caring what she dished up for me and tonight I was eating cheese. Just a block of cheddar, and tomorrow it would be tapioca pudding. It wouldn't matter how much of the cheese or the pudding, but I'd decided I could only have one thing.

My brother and sisters chewing quietly around me and the clock ticking and me so excited about that cheese, but so scared of it touching anything else because then I'd have to skip my next meal, and soon I'd begin restricting how much of that one thing, and Mum would force cod liver oil and Dad would ground me for a week but they couldn't make me eat.

Because if I didn't eat, I didn't feel so sad. I finally mattered for the numbers on the scale; I felt like I counted, even as I felt all my ribs before bed, even when I could no longer run or walk or hold a bat.

And that's when the counselors asked Dad if he knew what my favorite color was, if he could describe my likes and dislikes, if he knew what my dreams were, and my father—who knew everyone in the church and community—said no.

He didn't know.

At the end of every day, it's time to make supper.

Our house has a renovated kitchen with a walk-in pantry and a wide island where I can set Aiden and he eats pieces of apple and tomato. He helps me stir, dumps in cups of flour that dusts his freckled nose. Shakes cinnamon and puts his dimpled hand on mine, and together we break the eggs. "I twy, I twy," he says, and so he tries, the shell falling like tiny pieces of paper.

I was the girl who ate crackers throughout university, who snacked on marshmallows, and now I have two hungry boys and a man to feed.

I was the girl who would suck in her ribs and her cheeks and I sometimes dream of a daughter, one with pink ribbons in her hair. But I wouldn't know how to feed her.

"Em—can we dump half of that back?" Trent says, nodding at the bowl of tomato soup I've poured for Aiden. "I want Aiden to be able to finish his supper, to make the end attainable."

"I don't want your help," I say, like the sinner I am—because I want to be normal, weeps the nine-year-old into her pillow every night while her stomach growls.

I just want to be good enough.

Another night Trent gently takes the plate of spaghetti I've dished out for Aiden and spoons some of it back into the pot. "He'll never eat all of that," he says, and again I choke.

Trent's not being mean, he's saying this because he wants his children to learn the satisfaction of finishing their supper, but I take it personally. Because I still don't know correct portion size. And I am so afraid of my children starving that I'm overfeeding them.

I was thirteen in Richard's Landing on St. Joseph Island with its maple sugar candy and the fish and chips shop at the wharf, white boats flocking like seagulls, and the United Church where Dad preached just a block away from the coast.

In the basement of the church there was a table piled with food, a potluck, and three kinds of potatoes and seven kinds of salads, I know, because I was counting like some people count ceiling tiles, and I hadn't eaten since Saturday morning. There were sausages and buns, little tabs of butter, and the kids could line up first, so I took a plate and made it to the end of the line with just a few pickles that I later snuck into a napkin and put in the garbage.

I was sixty pounds and purple from hypothermia and admitted into the hospital the next day. I was so skinny I couldn't lose any more weight. I hadn't eaten in two days but my body was the same weight it had been two days earlier and Mum said I was a miracle and I pulled at my hair, another clump in my hands, my nails brittle.

This is what dying felt like—all scratchy and cold like this—and it smelled like Lysol.

They put a plate of food in front of me, heaped high, and my body didn't respond anymore because it was always responding— always growling, long into the night, sometimes so loud Mum would hear it in her bed and I looked at those mashed potatoes, the beef, the peas, and they said I could either pick up a fork and eat or they'd put an IV in me.

I picked up my fork and ate.

We've just finished supper and I'm clearing off the table—Marge made fried chicken and potatoes, boiled Brussels sprouts, coleslaw and white buns—and Trent on the couch, Kasher on Harvey's chest looking into his Opa's eyes and making bubbles, Aiden at the table drinking an orange float.

He is done now and Marge wipes his face with a warm wash-cloth. "Do you want some strawberries and ice cream?" she asks and he nods happily. When he has finished his strawberries she brings out the puzzles and they sit and fit the pieces together while she asks him questions like, "What's your favorite animal, Aiden?" and he says bunnies, and she exclaims over and over how smart he is as he completes the puzzle.

Harvey talks about Kasher's cute little hands and his bubbles and tells him stories about the deer he saw that day and laughs when Kasher grabs his nose.

Time. There is so much of it for everyone under this roof.

And my heart aches like a cold ice cube in the bottom of a glass, because it is so beautiful, the way they love, and I know why my husband has confidence in who he is. Why he hikes up his pajama pants in the middle of the living room and dances for the world to see, why he never has trouble sleeping and never questions his purpose because "I like myself," he says. "I don't care what other people think."

Trent grew up in a home across the yard from his grandmother, on the farm his Papa started and his dad took over, and his yard holds memories. His room still whispers secrets about the little boy who would stay up reading under his blankets with a flashlight. The aluminum shed out back holding baseballs and bats and bikes from his childhood, his garden bursting with strawberry plants as old as his skin, and he can tell stories about the games of soccer he played in the hallway with his dad.

His Papa did magic tricks when he was still alive. Papa had been a man who made bullets in the kitchen, the attic full of birds and stray animals the kids brought in—the scratch of foot and the brush of wing against the rafters—and that says a lot about Grandma Wierenga, who made the best white buns in the district and bowled higher scores than her grandchildren.

Grandpa Neumann ran the ferry and most Sundays after church they'd go to Grandma Neumann's for lunch, for pots of coffee and roast beef dinners and the cousins watching television in the sunken living room.

Trent would wake at four in the morning with his mom and trudge through the snow, his dad pulling calves from their mothers' wombs into the cold dawn, and him rubbing the calves' wet bodies with straw, urging their lungs to take a breath and leading them to their mamas for milk, their spindly legs still wet from birth.

Every spring he and his cousins would float sticks down the creek and float the runoff in canoes or on homemade rafts, the cows watching with the lazy flick of a tail in the new green of the meadow. He would race Grandma Wierenga to find the first strawberry of the season and the first cob of corn, and play a game he invented with a bat and two rain barrels called Canadian Cricket in the grass with his sisters.

Fall would bring the harvest, the air smelling of canola chaff and dust and sweat, bottles of frozen water in the freezer and iced tea in the fridge for the long Indian summer days in a combine. Trent and his cousins running through the fields, playing tag in the rows, riding beside Harvey above the waves of green—the sun on their backs, pushing, guiding, and you could see the years lengthen, even as the crops were cut.

And family picnics across the river, riding the old Vega ferry—getting out of the car on the way across and competing for balance on the rails; driving across the sand hills to find the largest leaf, to jump down the sandy slopes.

It's life on a farm, which shuts down on Sundays—tractors dotted across the Neerlandian landscape like pauses in a sentence—to resume on Monday after two church services, Sunday dinner and a nap.

"Who are we, without family?" Trent says one night as we make the drive home.

Kasher asleep in his car seat, Aiden in his pajamas, the fields scrolling by. Long plots of tired dirt, waiting for winter.

I nod beside him, there in the dark.

A tear on my cheek.

PART 2

Wife

To be fully seen by somebody, then, and be loved anyhow—
this is a human offering that can border on miraculous.

Elizabeth Gilbert

5

Dreadlocks

There is nothing more admirable than when two people who see eye to eye keep house as man and wife, confounding their enemies and delighting their friends.

Homer

November 2011

Trent's mom is going to lose her hair.

The kitchen smells of coffee and Grandma Neumann's apple squares on the table. Auntie Susan is over—Harvey's sister-in-law who's slim and blonde and does triathlons—and she is trimming the grandbabies' hair, five grandsons ages five and under.

I visit with Trent's sisters on the couch and Marge is sweeping up the hair even as it falls. "I'm not so scared of dying, but don't make me lose my hair!" she says with a shaky laugh, and all of us women touch the backs of our heads.

I've been maturing my dreads for two years. I got them right before we conceived Aiden, right before our trip to New York

City where we watched *Chicago* and ate pretzels in Central Park. A hairdresser gave them to me after I did a mural on the wall of her salon. She backcombed my hair into sections then smeared in beeswax and they didn't look like much in the beginning. None of us really do.

But I kept backcombing them and smearing in beeswax and slept with my hair in a kerchief and then one day they looked like they knew what they were becoming. I washed them with tea tree oil shampoo and the dreads began to cling to each other, like hundreds of thin arms intertwined, and I looked bohemian with my stretched ears.

It took a couple of years for the dreads to mature, to thicken into ropes, and I was growing into them even as they grew on me.

And then Marge talked about her hair. About how she was going to miss it when the chemo took it, and I've never really known how to help her.

I knew how to take care of my own Mum, who had brain cancer. By washing her feet and cooking her meals and making her bed and singing to her even as she lay there, hours on end, a crimson blanket tacked over the window.

But Marge isn't that sick and all she wants from me is a visit. She wants to take care of me. "That's the greatest gift you can give her," Trent says, when I try to buy her presents. "Just let her make you a cup of coffee."

When we first moved here, there were men in our house, upstairs and outside, installing our woodstove because we've always wanted to make our own heat, and there was hammering and feet in our attic and wood crumbs and drills boring holes. Aiden had a fever and a runny nose and I was trying to keep him quiet downstairs but finally I called Marge, who lives a country mile down the road, and she said, "Come over! Stay as long as you need to, of course! I'm so glad you asked."

Why is it always so hard to ask?

It felt so good to sit on her couch that day in the quiet of her home, the walls covered in photo frames of family. Her making a bed for Aiden and telling me to rest. "I've got it—you need a break," she said, and my whole body said *thank you*.

We ate homemade vegetable cream soup and fresh bread with strawberry jam and it was so quiet, the sound of the wind outside through the twenty-year-old evergreens.

There's rarely a supper Marge doesn't invite Grandma Wierenga over from the other yard, and she often brings a pot of garden potatoes. Grandma Neumann's vehicle is parked in the driveway three days a week for coffee. Marge took care of her father until he passed away and now she's attentive to both her mothers, doing family better than anyone I know.

Because home is not the house we live in but the people whose pictures line the walls. Whose clothes sit piled on the dryer. Whose dishes sit waiting to be washed. And making a home is a daily sacrifice of creating and holding and being.

"None of us knows how long we've got," Marge says, setting another place at the table. "Some days it's hard, but God has called us to take care of each other, and he will take care of us."

We are told to wash our feet in the bucket on the back step on hot summer days before we enter Marge's house, because clean floors are next to godliness in her mind. And the table's always laden with food, bowls of cooked carrots with butter, pan-fried fish, tiny potatoes, taco salad, and for dessert—home-canned peaches.

And I wish I hadn't said no to her at my wedding.

It was the day before the ceremony, and we were standing outside my parents' house in the sun, a white tent erected in the middle of the lawn and the trellis climbing with roses. I was sweating in a tank top and Marge asked if she could invite some relatives to the reception the next day, and Mum and I had already planned the seating arrangement, had fought over the seating arrangement, and Mum was lying down a lot with headaches because the tumor was growing.

So I said, "It's just too much right now." And Marge walked away sad. Because she never says no to anyone who wants a meal or a bed or the coat off her back, and she's taught me it's easy enough to pull up another chair and people don't need much. Just make them a sandwich, she says, pour them a cup of coffee and listen to their stories.

I'm listening to Marge's stories, now, how she grew up in the tiny German town of Vega five miles down the highway, how she used an outhouse until she was ten, how the house got so cold her blankets would be covered in frost and sometimes mice would run across her feather tick.

Ever since the day when Trent first brought me home, when I accidentally smashed Marge's chandelier with my fist playing Dutch Blitz and Marge laughed and said, "Thank goodness! I've been wanting an excuse to buy a new kitchen light!" she's shown me a kind of love the world has forgotten.

She never gave up on me. Even those three years when I starved myself, and then she flew out to Korea to visit us because she loved us enough to cross an ocean. When I gave birth to my eldest she came out to Ontario and slept on a cot in the front porch of our tiny one-bedroom house in November—for three weeks. Watched movies with me on the couch, cooked us meals, and kissed my cheeks when I said I couldn't do it, told me she believed I could.

And it was both of my mothers praying for me—back when I was drinking twelve cups of coffee a day and only eating supper and refusing to have children—it was their prayers that family would become important to me that saved me.

And it's their prayers that are bringing me home, now, to my sons.

Marge has taught me that we're all family, that we love until it hurts, that when God gives us a husband and children, home-making becomes our calling. She's taught me that there's as much dignity in reading bedtime stories to one's children as in reading the *New York Times*, that there's as much value in hugging a small child as in writing a book, that having my name on the cover of a bestseller is not near so important as having God's name on my lips.

"Are you scared, Mom?"

Auntie Susan is gone now, the hair all swept up, and Trent's sisters are laying their boys down for a nap. I am in the kitchen with Marge, and we've been visiting a lot these days because her chemo will start soon and she'll be living in the city with the girls.

Marge is taking dishes out of the dishwasher; the teakettle is on and Aiden is watching *Flintstones* in the living room.

Marge turns to me. She is young, only fifty-two, Harvey eight years her senior, and she is slim with bright eyes and a quick smile. Before she got married at eighteen, she used to barrel race and goat tie in the rodeo.

"No, I'm not scared," she says. "Just sad, because, well, I won't be home to take care of Harvey, and you know, Emily . . ." and she pauses here, looks over at her husband who's fixing a bulb that's burned out. He'll fix anything she asks him to, and some days he brings in clusters of wildflowers from the field for her. "He's my ministry. He always has been. The kids are important too of course, but I have always felt my first calling is to serve my husband."

She says this with a smile, even as she bends and continues to unload the dishwasher.

I want to bend and serve this way.

But I've been angry so long.

At men mostly, and I was the little girl who would watch her dad talking to everyone at church, laughing with them, wondering what they had that she didn't. Because the laughter stayed at church. Dad slipped straight to his desk at home, and I would knock timidly at his door and he'd sigh, push up his glasses, and ask what I wanted. He was about God's business and I was in the way.

So I stopped eating and then I started yelling, and I would scream, "I hate you!" when Dad grounded me because I refused to eat supper and then I'd punch him. And he'd let me. Because he loved me more than I could understand then, in a way that refused to erupt in anger even when I deserved it.

It's hard to call God *father*.

Because the little girl in me still needs her dad to look up from his desk and see her. And Marge talks about serving Harvey like it's something holy and privileged, and I can only swallow and look away.

There are days when I weep for the unraveling. The clothesline an endless string of diapers and baby sleepers and Trent and I arguing over how to properly pin a shirt and then Aiden falls on Kasher and it takes everything in me to keep my voice calm for the sadness in his tiny face. Because he didn't mean to hurt his baby brother.

There is so much sadness to love, and it's so easy to hurt the one who holds you. To squeeze too tight or let go too soon, and I escape to the garden Marge helped me plant, the one at the corner of the house with poppies and daisies and sweet peas, a quiet, windless place where the stems grow tall and strong. And I can be alone, for just a while.

And it's there, unraveling with the weeds, that I remember them. The five children Trent pointed out to me on Sunday, the ones trailing behind their father into church, their backs bent, hands in pockets.

They'd all just lost their mother. A sudden death, a brain aneurism. And I'd stared, never having seen them before. And somehow they walked into church, and they shook the hands of the Sunday greeters and they made it to the pew where they'd sat weeks earlier grieving the loss of the one who gave them life.

That's all I needed to turn my feet back toward the house, back into the arms of my husband and my children, for I would fold a thousand diapers just to hold my loved ones for another hour.

This is love, isn't it? With all of its grief, with all of its clotheslines and potty training and wedded misunderstanding.

And this is what's worth living and dying for.

"There's so little time," Marge tells me. "I just don't want to waste it."

Marge has cancer but she's also got more life than most of us.

In ancient times, stars were used as navigational guides, to lead people home. I once heard that stars are balls of fire that break off and become brighter in the breaking.

Marge is brighter for the breaking. And her light is leading me home.

Trent and I stand in front of the bathroom mirror together, me clipping off my dreadlocks and him shearing his head into a crew cut. He holds the razor and me the scissors, and Aiden stands in the doorway watching as the floor becomes littered with hair.

I don't cry. I don't go bald either; I leave a couple of inches and it's not the first time I've worn a boy cut. Mum used to give me one when I was knee-high. And in Korea, my friend Stasha cut off my hair because it was splitting from the bleach, and now here I am again.

"It's just hair," Trent says, looking at the bathroom floor. "It will grow back."

We drive to the farm that night, with our sons and our shorn hair. Passing fields of snow, the sky like a smoldering match, we step into the house that always smells like cinnamon buns and every room is filled with light.

We peel our shoes quietly on the mat, step toward the kitchen where Marge is visiting with Grandma Wierenga over mugs of tea and she looks up. "Oh, my goodness!" she says.

"We want you to know you're not alone, Mom," Trent says.

Marge doesn't cry often.

But her eyes are wet when she touches our heads.

"Thank you," she whispers.

6

Broken Doorbells

Normal day, let me be aware of the treasure you are. Let
me learn from you, love you, bless you before you depart.

Mary Jean Irion

November 2011

I'm a mess on the massage table.

A candle flickering, making flowers on the walls, stems and
petals all painted with fire. The sound of the ocean on the stereo
and the masseuse's hands on my neck.

It's Friday and Trent is home with the boys while I'm here smelling incense and oils.

"Do you drink enough water?" The masseuse's hands are warm.
I don't.

"Water helps the knots to dissolve and these ones are just not
wanting to go," she says. "I've never seen anyone so tight—has
anything stressful happened lately?"

There had been my friend wanting to abort another child, junior high girls cutting themselves and me visiting them in the hospital, Trent and the boys sick, and me trying to finish the novel, the one that will make me someone.

"Just relax," she says, turning my neck.

My head won't move.

"I'm sorry," I say.

"It's okay," she says. "I'll just keep reminding you, and you just keep trying."

I nod.

The other day I stepped from the bathroom combing my hair; it was ten in the morning and I'd showered and dressed, and Trent was still in his pajamas. It was Saturday, and he didn't have to teach.

He came up to me, put his arms around me. "You look sexy," he said, and I shook my head. "Not now."

I checked my email then and he followed me, put his arms on my shoulders. I shrugged, went outside where Aiden was playing in the snow, called him in. Because all of a sudden it was time to have lunch, I'd decided, and Trent went quietly away. Aiden came quietly inside.

And everything sort of quietly grieved.

I'd missed it. I'd missed intimacy.

"Remember to breathe," the masseuse says, now.

Her fingers pressing on a knot, shooting pain. "Breathing loosens the pressure, and helps things to flow," she says. "Our first instinct is to stop breathing when we're in pain, but it doesn't help."

I draw in air, let it out, stare at the wall, at the candle and flame, at the stems and petals, breathing in and out like I'm giving birth in a field of flowers.

The pain passes and she is moving my neck, saying, "There, it's so much more pliable now."

I don't want to leave. I need her to teach me, but the forty-five minutes are up.

She leaves and I get dressed. Take a moment to brush my two inches of hair, spray on some perfume. I move my neck back and forth, slow my steps even as I pay and walk to the car. I purchase a bottle of water for my drive home. It is sunny, the sky like a field of daffodils.

I get home and the first thing I do is hug Trent.

We hold each other, the boys downstairs laughing.

"Everything okay?" Trent says into my hair.

I nod.

Love takes time, sunshine, rain, weeding. There is no hurry in love, only waiting and resting. Like a plant, stretching.

"Thank you for loving me," I say.

It's the hardest thing for me to believe—that he could.

"I've never stopped," he says.

I remember when he started.

That hot day back in 2003, in the tufts of my parents' lawn, the roses climbing the white trellis, wild, and Trent and I signing the registry while my brother, sister, and friend sang next to the flower garden.

Mum in her violet dress, the folding chairs, and Dad in a smart black suit standing beside me, and me just wanting to run.

I was the girl who did five years of high school in four because I couldn't wait to catch the bus out west, forty hours from home, when I turned eighteen.

There's a wedding photo on my desk, and in it, Trent is on one knee and I am in my empire-waist dress, a rim of flowers around my blonde hair. It's black and white, which is fitting, because those years held no color.

I painted in the attic of our cozy home on a corner lot while I starved myself again, because I didn't know how to be a wife, and Dad and Mum visited us three years into my marriage, three years into my relapse, three years into punching holes in the walls and painting them over with bright latex and drinking too much and eating too little and putting doilies on the coffee table.

They flew out west and we sat in a circle in our living room with its doilies and its yellow walls and its purple couch.

"I'm so sorry I wasn't there for you, Emily," Dad said, pushing up his glasses and Mum nodding beside him. "Can you forgive me?"

Dad held my hand that afternoon, spring light pooling in through the window, the smell of apple blossoms wafting in through the backdoor screen.

And I looked at him and for the first time I really saw him—this handsome man with the kind eyes whose DNA coursed through my stubborn, compassionate genes, and I saw a man who loved me enough to spend money on an airplane ticket, who had realized, through counseling and prayer, the pain a pastor's kid can go through.

Dad loved me enough to say sorry.

I became my father's daughter that day.

And I wished to go back, somehow, to do my childhood all over again, with more grace this time.

We moved to Korea to teach English in the afternoons and sing karaoke and meet foreigners at pubs and travel to Japan and China and Thailand on our weekends off.

And nine months later, I learned how sick Mum was, and I flew home.

The houseplants dying, the laundry overflowing, dust on every ledge and book, and the Ping-Pong table piled thick with papers and boxes while Mum slept for days on end.

But Dad and I knelt together in the garden talking and praying together, and when Mum was awake she hugged me and told me I was beautiful, over and over, while I fed her soup or helped her get changed.

It wasn't pretty, and I felt the calluses on Mum's feet when I cut her nails, but her smile was soft.

Our spirits grappled. We became human, together, needing each other. Dad and I would lift Mum from her bed and change her together and Mum washed my feet one day and she would lean on me and dance to worship music.

It's in leaning on humanity that we glimpse the divine.

And I've glimpsed it.

And now Mum is better; her tumor is gone and doctors are shaking their heads and Trent and I have two boys and we've moved out west, to a tiny town north of Edmonton, Alberta, to live near the farm. Near Trent's parents, and we moved into a house in the hamlet.

A house with a broken doorbell and a dirty mat.

I glance out the kitchen window, at the temperature gauge covered in snow. Catch sight of Trent biking home as he does every day, carving ruts with his wheels, his blue school bag across his back and I rush to the door. Open it, a gasp of cold in my face, and I wait.

Hear the slide of the garage door and the steps of him approaching, and there he is.

My husband. Frost on his goatee, a smile in his eyes.

"Hi, honey," I say. "Welcome home."

7

Kleenex

The darker the night, the brighter the stars. The deeper the grief, the closer is God!

Fyodor Dostoyevsky

December 2011

I am running the long stretch of country mile, north of Neerlandia, past the red silos, the farms silent in the cold.

Christmas is in one week, but celebration feels lost with Marge soon to be undergoing chemo treatments.

I want to gather up the sunlight and bring it home to Trent. A basketful of gold, an offering of happy in the darkness of these days, but it will take more than a basket.

Trent is grieving. He can't fix his mom in the same way he couldn't fix his wife when she was starving herself, and it's hard for him to let anything be broken.

And most of the time I can't tell he's sad, my six-foot husband with long legs and broad shoulders, with eyes that smile and the kindest lips, who takes Aiden in the old farm truck, painted blue and red, into the woods behind his parents' farm to cut down trees.

My man who smells like sawdust, who believes "wood smoke should be bottled as a cologne," who eats lime chips and salsa with me every night, our feet sticking out from beneath our afghan as we watch Netflix.

But as he draws me close at night, beneath the quilt, I can feel his heart through his skin; I feel his sorrow: the unexplained sadness of a mother turning sick, and him not knowing how to help. My husband is the man who cannot bear his mom replacing the living room carpet or the light fixture in the kitchen and now he's suddenly facing a much bigger change: cancer.

And so we hold each other beneath the sheets and I bite my lip for wanting to help him, in the same way that he wants to help his mom, and all of us being so very mortal.

And sometimes the greatest help we can offer is a quiet touch. The assurance that, *Baby, I cannot change what's happening but I can sit here with you in the middle of what's happening, and no matter what happens, I will not leave you.*

Him, in my arms, and me being able to offer myself, and every time we unite in the middle of sorrow, it's our wedding vows.

And I do this now too, choosing my husband in the middle of his night, in the middle of his grief. Because Trent has walked my grief with me. He walked through my mum's brain cancer, through three years of Mum trying to lift a fork to her mouth at our thrift-store table and falling asleep on our secondhand leather couch, carrying Mum to the car because she couldn't walk, letting me visit Mum and Dad day after day to clean and fold their laundry and help Mum get dressed and remember how to use the DVD player.

So now it's my turn. To walk with him. Because we all take our turns.

"Are you scared?" I say to him, then, in bed. It is midnight but neither of us is sleeping.

Trent looks at me. His unshaven face, his hazel eyes. "I just never thought it would happen to her," he says. "You just think your mom is, well, invincible. Moms aren't supposed to get hurt."

I nod.

"I know," I say.

He kisses the top of my shorn head and we meet there in the middle of the sagging mattress.

But then some nights, we can't.

We have one set of bed sheets, and they're tattered for the washing. In the winter it's a feather tick we sleep under, feathers plucked by the Hutterites who live down the road from us.

I cry because it's our wedding night all over again—two sons later.

"Shhh—it's okay, Em, we'll try again," he says. But I know it's not just my body that won't surrender.

We sleep beneath the feathers, and some nights, Trent kicks it off because he's too hot. He wears no clothes to bed and me, wrapped in flannels, and "You should really try sleeping naked," Trent says, holding me. "You'd be so much warmer."

"I doubt that," I say with a laugh. "I know why you want me to though!"

We laugh and then he kisses my neck. "You know, sometimes, Em, I just want to hold you."

I nod. I know. Because he is the man who waited six months just to kiss me. Who waited twenty-three years to be intimate with someone—and that someone was me, on our wedding night.

But I was sewn tight that night, and the champagne didn't loosen anything. Trent waiting in the bed in the cottage, his black suit and white shirt flung on the floor and him leaning on one arm. The July heat whispering through a window, and the beach just steps from the cottage. The stars like the crystals on my dress, clustered together, and I thought about running.

"Are you coming, Em?" Trent said, and I let that dress fall, clutching the sheets to my flat chest and he pulled me close but I was an aged envelope that had glued shut. Him saying, "Babes, it's okay, we have our whole lives to figure this out."

We were the couple who, when we were dating, hadn't been able to stop kissing until three in the morning, but now, after the vows beneath the trellis and my dad's tender prayer and the rose petals falling, now that we were married, I was like a caged bird. Him trying to open the lock but I wanted that cage. I knew every corner, every rung, and I'd put myself in there when I was sixteen.

Trent has fallen asleep against my shoulder, his quiet snores in my ear, his long arms around my waist.

I'm reading *And the Mountains Echoed* by Khaled Hosseini, my bedside table littered with earplugs and sleeping pills. And some nights, still, even after two babies and ten years of becoming one beneath the sheets, my body still runs to that cage. I'm that bird learning how to fly, because it's not easy for this woman who's been hurt to pull off her underwear—the white bunchy kind with loose elastic, like a wilted flower.

I refused to pull them off for Levi. I was sixteen, and Levi's house was short and square, sitting on a lonely plot of land in Northern Ontario, and we rode the school bus together, his dad meeting us at the door with a bottle of beer in his hands. His mom had left years earlier and the kitchen showed this: piles of plates and glasses by the sink, newspapers on chairs and dust on counters.

Levi was captain of the basketball team. He took me to his living room first, a long uncomfortable couch on the wall, a television in the center of the room and smeared windows. Outside on the lawn, a broken trampoline with snapped springs.

We watched *Wheel of Fortune* and he found my neck. Then our bodies found the floor, and he peeled himself up, took me to his room that smelled of cologne, the blind across his window. Posters of supermodels on the walls, of Pamela Anderson and women in their underwear or nothing at all, and I lay on his bed, his wiry body on top of me, and he was trying to find my bra. What he found instead was the Kleenex, white bunches stuffed inside it because anorexia had eaten my chest.

I didn't look at him, and his fingers found other curves but I wouldn't let him unbutton my jeans. Soon we were coughing awkwardly and standing up, fidgeting with our shirts and he left me in the room, got himself a glass of water. This husky-voiced boy with the laughing eyes, and he took me to a bush party that night. I drank nothing and kept checking my watch, sitting beside him at the bonfire and everyone glancing at this pastor's daughter in the Value Village coat and the long blonde hair.

He broke up with me the next day in the courtyard of the school. "It's just, you're too nice," he said, and I nodded. Bit my bottom lip and he smiled, put his hand on my cheek. "I'm sorry," and he walked away, his pants hanging low, and I gripped the bench so I wouldn't chase after him.

Mum bought me roses. Brought them to me in my bedroom in the basement and the thorns made my fingers bleed and I leaned on her shoulder. Sobbed. "Too nice, Mum, he said I was too nice. I thought nice was a good thing."

Mum shook her head, held my hand. "No, honey, it's not what you think," she said in her British accent. "Too nice means you refused to go all the way with him." She touched my silver purity ring on my wedding finger. "I'm proud of you, Emily."

Mum smelled like Jergens lotion. The roses left pink dust on my skin and even after she closed the door I sat there, thorns pricking my fingers.

Dad was still at the office. He drove one and a half hours twice a week to work a part-time job at a church in Goulais River, staying overnight midweek, and by the time he got home the roses would be in a vase on my desk and I'd be brushing my teeth in the bathroom. The tiny one at the end of the hall, and Dad had built a makeshift shower in the laundry room where he'd installed a gauge to measure how much water we used.

I wouldn't tell him. He'd peck my cheek in the morning as usual, ask me how I was, and I'd say "fine" and he'd measure out his bowl of homemade granola and skim milk, and we'd sit side by side at the breakfast table. He'd met Levi; I'd brought him over on the bus one afternoon and told him not to swear in front of my parents and Mum had made chicken and rice. Dad had asked Levi about basketball and school, and my brother and sisters had giggled behind their hands.

But Dad and I sat in silence that morning, him reading his *Daily Bread* devotional and our dogs making more conversation than us, whimpering and barking in the basement, shuffling toward their dishes of food, and I heard the thump of Christy, our black collie, lying down to eat because she was arthritic.

And then we both rinsed our dishes and slid them into the sink to be washed by whoever's turn it was that night—because the dishwasher, we'd been taught, used $0.75 in water each load—and I went to the bathroom, looked in the mirror at my red eyes. Washed my face. Put on my makeup. Rode the bus to school.

And somewhere on that ride between the backwoods of Echo Bay, past the grey slate of Highway 17, all maples budding green, and to the high school in Desbarats, Ontario, I thought about Levi, and the Kleenex, about Dad at the breakfast table and the silence in between, and I looked out the window, at the asphalt—dark like syrup, the warm kind we poured onto snow and turned into toffee—and in that moment, my wings were clipped.

Poet Maya Angelou writes of this, the free bird who leaps on the back of the wind, who floats downstream, who dips his wing in the orange sun and dares to claim the sky. But, she says, a bird who lives in his narrow cage can seldom see through the bars for the rage. His wings clipped, his feet tied. So instead, he opens his throat to sing.

I'd spend the next seven years singing freedom without ever leaving that cage and when a kind farm boy from Neerlandia pulled me to him the night of our wedding, for all of his warm hands and soft lips, I found myself back on that school bus.

A sixteen-year-old girl clutching her backpack, afraid of being burned by the sun.

8

Mountains

You care so much you feel as though you will bleed to death with the pain of it.

J. K. Rowling

December 2011

There's a small fake tree with popcorn strings and lights blinking red, blue, and green at eight in the morning.

The couches are full, the sisters and their babies and Trent in the chair, me holding Aiden in his Thomas the Train pajamas, a sticky candy cane in his small hand, and Marge and Harvey still in bed because they're waiting.

Waiting for "On the First Day of Christmas," and Teneale starts in her strong alto. She has her father's voice, and Trent's bass is Neumann loud, the kind that blurts out "Five golden rings" with resounding vibrato, and Aiden stares at his daddy while the rest of us laugh. Teshah blends in with her sweet soprano, and Marge and

Harvey wait in bed until we sing a few more songs. It's a tender morning here, because of Marge's recent two surgeries and, after Christmas, the chemo.

But here she comes finally, in her bathrobe and her skin not as flush, but she's still able to pick up Aiden and kiss his cheeks and ask who wants coffee.

Normally by Christmas Marge would have spent months frying bacon and cooking lasagnas and pizzas to pull out, and the freezer would be bulging with Oh Henry squares and currant tarts, but this year Teshah's brought out finger food.

The presents are piled by the tree, crowding out the tree, and "Kasher, don't eat that, honey," because paper is already in his mouth, and a smile on his face.

There are tubs full of socks and gift certificates from Marge and Harvey for the adults—but the kids go first. All five of them taking turns handing out the gifts, "Now, Aiden, you had Logan's name, so can you give this one to him?", and then the scramble and rush of ripping and laughing.

And through it all Marge and Harvey sitting together on the floor in their bathrobes, holding each other, watching their grandbabies. Clapping and laughing, and in spite of cancer the room pulses with life.

I pick up the discarded paper while Trent and his sisters line the kitchen counter, as though they're six, nine, and eleven again, and Marge gives them the crescent dough and they roll it and put it in the oven. They make icing and soon we're eating the soft warm pastries.

Later the grandmas will come over and we'll have pancakes and eggs and bacon, and Grandma Wierenga will pull out Wizard—a trick-taking card game—and Marge will bring out the chocolates and rippled chips and dip.

But I catch her with wet eyes, in the middle of things.

And we all pause for a minute, then talk extra loud. "Dad, have you seen any deer lately?" Trent calls to Harvey who's looking at his camera, there on the floor.

Harvey grins, beckons Trent over, shows him photo after photo of the deer he feeds and photographs in the bush and it's a dance, this way of doing family. This pulling out songs and gifts and life amid the grief.

And sometimes I catch Marge hugging her grandbabies extra-long, and there are no plans anymore. We don't make schedules, we just thank Jesus for today, for life, for this moment.

"Settlers, anyone?" Trent pulls out the toolbox holding his game pieces. And we play as we always have—lots of yelling and arm-jabbing between Teshah and Trent, and Teneale groaning and me rolling my eyes; Mom asks Trent to move her pieces for her because she's feeding one of the kids and visiting with the grandmas.

Then it's a sled ride behind the snowmobile, out past the fields, to the evergreens. "See these prints, boys?" And Harvey shows the older boys the prints in the snow, of deer, and the sprinkling of oats—he's brought buckets more—and the old rusted truck cab is out here, still, where he sometimes sits and watches wildlife.

We pile sticks and Trent starts a fire. Mom has forgotten the smokies but we've got wieners and buns, and the little boys sit in plastic chairs while we roast.

It's quiet enough to hear the love being passed with the marsh-mallows and cups of hot chocolate, a love of Jesus that whispers, *Nothing—not life or death, nor any kind of cancer, nor angels or demons nor the present or the future—can separate us.*

Soon, we're piling back into the sled and the snowmobile and the truck, the children under blankets and the babies sleeping, and it's home because Marge is tired—and we drive back to our house, to the tall pine we chose weeks earlier, decorated with childhood ornaments, to the toy train that Aiden turns on and off, on and off.

And Trent and I sit quietly on the couch, Kasher asleep in our laps, watching Aiden and the train, which we pull out once a year to run on a track around our tree; Christmas slowly comes to an end—like a solo ballerina and her final pirouette, applause, and the curtain falls. The audience rising to go brush teeth and slip into bed.

A week later, we pack up the Subaru one afternoon, Mom insisting on taking the boys while she can, and we drive to Jasper to go snowboarding. To the tall Rockies, to the Indian Head, to the frozen rivers and Maligne Canyon.

We pick up Chinese takeout and some beer, and we head to our room, above an old shop—where we dump our stuff everywhere, turn on the TV, eat side by side on one of the double beds, our wool socks touching—and Trent's have a hole.

When the food is done, our fingers smelling like ginger beef, we pull out the cards and play poker, and then it's bed.

"I'm scared—what if I fall on my face? What if I forget how to board down the mountain?" I say, pulling on my pajamas, and Trent laughs. "You say the same thing every year, and every year you're fine."

He taught me to snowboard when we first got married and it was three years of bruises before I stopped falling, before I started flying down the winding paths of white.

And I can't rest that night. Footsteps in the hall, muffled voices next to us, and for hours we lie there in our separate beds because the room came with two.

Finally, I start to cry. Trent stretches out his hand across the space between our beds, his fingers reaching for me in the dark. "Hold on to me, Em," he says. "I'm here."

And maybe the secret to all of life is to never stop reaching out in the dark. To never stop taking hold of each other's hands. To never let go.

Not even for a moment.

9

A Love Letter

I fell in love the way you fall asleep: slowly, and then all at once.

John Green

You always want me to sit on the roof with you.

I'm scared of heights but you tell me the view is so much better up there, by the drainpipe on the shingles.

"You can see across the hamlet, Em, to the fields and beyond, and I won't let you fall," you tell me, but I just smile from where I stand on the deck by the flower garden. Where I can't see a thing. Where it's safe.

I tell you that I trust you, but the roof is so high, what if I fall, and yet I really want to see the world from a bird's-eye view: the patches of canola, the brilliant quilt-like fields woven together. The farmers sewing crops all along the highway right next to our house and you won't let me fall, you say, but I can't seem to climb the ladder.

I don't even fly in my dreams.

You have flying dreams all the time.

And even though I say I don't believe that nothing scares you, it comforts me. Like a baby bird, I'm peeking over the nest, feeling braver watching you fly.

I like to imagine how it would feel to sit close to you on the roof, and hold your hand on top of the world, the smile on your face from knowing your wife believes in you, but I believe in fear more, and this has been our swan song. This fear.

"Are you happy?" you ask me later, on the couch, the fold-out one we chose together at The Brick because we like to put our feet up at the end of a long day. "I want to make you happy," you say.

"You do," I say. Because you're the only person who can make me laugh. The kind of laugh that gives me a bellyache.

But sometimes I still hurt you.

I get so angry some nights, I can't see anything except black-and-white dots in front of me and you're in my way. It doesn't happen very often, but I swing at you and you back up and I swing again and you grab my arms to keep me from doing anything and I can't see you, I just see a man. A man who doesn't always agree with me, who says the things I need to hear, like "You need to go to bed now, Emily," or "You care too much about the wrong things."

The healing service didn't work.

I was starving myself back then, seven years ago when you were staff at Young Life—which mentors troubled teens—and I volunteered with them too, every day, after eight hours of editing a Christian newspaper.

And you'd heard of a healing service and you thought maybe they could just cast those anorexic demons out of me and I didn't think so. But we went anyway, to inner-city Edmonton where missions and bars line the streets and prostitutes and old men with carts walk the sidewalks. Where I'd taken Young Life girls to hand out bouquets of red roses, where I'd gone to feed the hungry during my King's University days, and now I was here to get healed.

Only nothing happened.

The room smelled of wet socks and soup because it was minus twenty-five outside and strangers put their hands on me in the name of Jesus and I sat there with my eyes open. Because I'm scared of new places, and I'm scared of the dark, and I'm scared of losing anything familiar, like my eating disorder.

So we went home and I swung at you then too, when we got inside, because you were mad that it hadn't made me better, that no demons had come flying out of me, and I lay down, my stomach growling, on the purple couch in our living room.

"What happened to the girl I married?" you said, and I missed her too.

I'm eating now, again, and we have two boys that have your eyes, and you tell me when you think I'm getting too skinny. "There's not much to you," you say sometimes when we're lying together beneath the feather tick. And when I've had a loud day with a lot of people, or I've eaten too much chocolate or not enough meat, and I'm not able to sleep, you're always there for me, you're always there to pray for me at two in the morning, and you tell me, "Emily, just picture your mind as a room. A large, empty room, and in the middle of that room is a fire. A huge, roaring fire, and that's God. And anytime a thought or worry tries to enter the room, throw it into the fire and let God consume it."

You're always there.

You wait for me every night to finish writing on the laptop so we can hang out, so we can play a board game or cards or watch a show. You come home from school and let me go on a run because you see that I need quiet and you still make me fancy salads for supper.

You grate the carrot and chop the onion that makes your eyes sting and you barbecue burgers, and I eat it, every last bite. And you get upset if I let anything go cold because you want me to enjoy my food. "I don't want to lose you," you say.

And I know you don't mean the anorexia, because I've been eating since that day in the car when you gave me the ultimatum.

But you mean lose me to my work, or to those demons that make me see black and white and swing at the air, and sometimes when I hurt you, you leave. You slam the door and get into our car, the kids asleep downstairs and our neighbors out, hand in hand, for their evening walk, and you leave without telling me where you're going and it feels like I'm falling. Right out of that nest, hard into night.

And I think of all the things I'll promise you when, and if, you come back, just please come back.

That's all you want for me too.

"When will the kids and I be enough for you?" you say, when I'm crying over some failed career attempt.

You smell like Speed Stick and you play hide-and-seek with the boys, bite their bellies and chase them, Kasher crawling and Aiden slipping in his socks.

You are my home, Trent. Whenever you bike to school in the morning, leaving me with toast crumbs and an empty milk glass and the boys, I feel a bit lost, and my compass, it points north when I hear you pulling open the garage door and parking your bike and walking to the house.

There's not a day when laundry isn't piled on our dryer; you slide it all into a basket and watch a hockey game while folding my underwear and the boys' tiny shirts. And then you go and chop firewood for an hour, the muscles in your arms flexing and you come in smelling like wood and you cook supper and I'm not sure why you need me.

But I need you like fireflies need light. I need you to tell me when enough is enough, to kill spiders for me, to read *Winnie the Pooh* to the kids while I catnap, to take us on quad rides across the wheat fields at Opa's, to pull me close under the covers. I need you to tell me to breathe deep and to stop staring at my laptop waiting for my prince to come because my prince is here, and it's you.

The same man who break-dances in the middle of my living room, who lies with me on the trampoline under the stars, and the other night you did this again. Aiden and Kasher were in bed, and you pulled our duvet out to the trampoline in the backyard, and our pillows, and then you told me to come with you and we lay there for about three minutes until I heard the boys crying.

So then we brought them out too, and we lay there, all four of us, on the trampoline counting the stars in the middle of summer. Talking about God and how he knows each star by name.

And on my birthday you baked me a carrot cake; you grated the carrots till your fingers nearly bled and you slathered it with cream cheese icing like Mum used to do, every year, cutting it into a house or the shape of a doll, and you did this even though I forgot your birthday.

I forgot it years ago when we were at camp with Young Life kids and we were in the van driving home and you weren't talking much. It was four o'clock in the afternoon and I asked you what was wrong. Then one of the leaders in the front said, "Hey, Trent—it's July fourth, isn't that your birthday, man?"

And you looked at me, and I saw everything I'd put you through, written clear across your handsome face: all those nights of not sleeping, those days of me crying and getting angry and not eating and then, I went and forgot your birthday.

"Oh no," I said. "Oh no . . ."

And you shook your head.

I was sure we were over.

What did we have to hold on to, then?

But you found my hand, even then, my skinny, cold hand. And you held on.

I've been trying to make it up to you, since. I've been trying to throw surprise parties, which never work because I get too excited and tell you about them.

I remember this when you're gone, because when love walks out the door you stand there for a long time, watching the back of its head. Praying.

And hours later, you come back.

And I stand at the top of the stairs all swollen-eyed and whispering, "I'm sorry."

Thinking, *He came back. To me.*

It takes you awhile. You forgive me, slowly, but it will be days until you stop hurting because you love me that much, and I'm sorry. For making you sit in that car for hours, praying and staring out the window, finding the strength to turn around and drive home, and I ask why you married me. Why you married a woman who has panic attacks so bad they seize up her chest, who hates cooking and cleaning.

But you don't see that girl.

No, you see the girl I want to be. The one who cries whenever she has to leave on a trip because she's so afraid of messing up her sons.

You know my ups and downs and highs and lows and insides and outsides. You know my freckles in the summer, and that I love a cold Rickard's Red. You know I smoke cigars on occasion but will never smoke a cigarette because my Nanny could barely talk for all of the tar in her lungs. You know I don't know how to order from a menu and that I think I like salmon but really I just wish I liked salmon. You know I'm an introvert who shrinks if she's around too many people too long, that I laugh at puns and get mad at off-color jokes. And you don't want me to dye my hair because you like my natural color.

"You're the only one," I say.

And I love when you sing to me. I love when you make up songs in your off-tune voice and you croon about bacon (because it's your first love, next to me). I love when you pull me onto your lap and we watch a funny YouTube video together. I love that you're my friend.

And whenever we can, when the kids are asleep, we slip out to the garden. "Let's see how our children are growing," you say, and by children you mean our tomatoes and carrots and peas.

We weed the strawberries in the moonlight. We eat some fresh peas.

We walk the rows.

I want to have the kind of marriage that makes our kids want to get married.

And I want every woman to have a man like you.

The kind of man who never stops loving, who never stops believing, who never stops reaching for his wife's hand even when she's forgotten the day he was born, and this is forgiveness: the greatest gift, this for-giving, and you give it in abundance.

I will never stop being yours, Trent.

Forever, your girl with the straw-gold hair.

PART 3

Mother

Sometimes when you pick up your child you can feel the map of your own bones beneath your hands, or smell the scent of your skin in the nape of his neck. This is the most extraordinary thing about motherhood—finding a piece of yourself separate and apart that all the same you could not live without.

Jodi Picoult

10

Fostering

No one has ever become poor by giving.

Anne Frank

January 2012

We are downstairs by the woodstove, the fire making its warm, crackling sound—like children stepping on bubble wrap—and Kasher jumping in the jolly jumper, six months old; me, reading in the blue recliner. Trent on the floor stacking blocks with Aiden; the phone rings.

We let it ring a couple of times. I slowly reach for the cordless. "Hello?"

It's Ashley, a girl I met ten years ago through Young Life. I lost track of her for a while, but learned recently that she had two small boys and had taken them with her when she left her boyfriend after he'd pushed her down the stairs. She was trying to juggle school while finding a place for her and the boys to live. And life was unraveling.

"I can't do it," she says, crying into the phone. "I can't do it anymore, Emily. I can't be a mom."

I swallow. It's the same thing I've thought about myself a thousand times.

"You don't understand," this single mother says now, in a hiccupping whisper. "I'm a wreck. I just need some time, you know? To sort things out."

I tell her it's normal, that every mom feels this way. "No, Emily, this is bad. Trust me, I'm not a good person right now."

I ask her to take a few days and pray about what she wants to do, and then call me back.

"Okay," she says.

But even as I hang up the phone I know I need to go into the city. I need to bring those boys home.

Aiden is telling me about his Duplo tower. "And dis gween," he says, pointing to the blocks, because he's learning his colors. He hasn't quite learned pink and purple and he isn't a big talker, but his words come slow and sure, like he's tasting them—running his tongue over the contours of nouns and vowels. Kasher chuckles and jumps, his short legs fat and strong. His face stretching full into smile.

Trent's eyes catch mine over the heads of our sons. "I'll make supper tonight," he says, because he knows.

The torn, exhausted look of someone trying to pull another person out of quicksand.

I drive into the city soon after that phone call, meet with Ashley and her sons.

"Those boys need our help," I tell Trent upon arriving home.

So we make space in our house for two more boys, for as long as we need to, until Ashley gets back on her feet.

I pray a lot. We are weak all around. Trent and I hug each other more than usual, and read piles of stories to our boys and one night Trent makes us popcorn for supper and we all sit and hold each other on the couch watching a movie.

Soon there will be double the number of snow boots in our entrance and double the beds and double the runny noses.

I never wanted to be a mother, growing up. Being a mom meant spending yourself, always. It meant sacrificing your body, all varicose veins and weary. It meant wiping noses and bottoms and putting Scooby-Doo Band-Aids on knees.

And now my heart has stretch marks.

I don't have time to figure out the answers. I just have time to make beds and find car seats, and God will take care of the rest.

Yahweh. Nothing surprises him, and even as we cling to each other he is making room for a miracle.

Days before the boys arrive we feed deer in the woods with Harvey. Trent's dad knows every antler; he's set up cameras to take their portraits. Sometimes he sits in the woods for hours, studying the deer, the way they interact, and he's built them a corral to keep the moose away.

We feed them and there is peace in the trees. In the sun and the sky and Aiden stepping carefully in the snow. And he leaves footprints, bigger than I've seen him leave and I know I need to follow. For he will lead me straight to the love I am looking for: the love that transcends my doubts.

And maybe it will all be easier than we thought.

The boys are coming. Trent is picking them up after his teachers' conference in the city and bringing them home—a two-hour ride from Edmonton to Neerlandia.

Their beds are ready. I bought them blankets, the fuzzy kind, the kind that makes you feel like you're being hugged in your sleep, and I bought one for Aiden too, because he'll notice if he doesn't have one, and I need to be extra careful about that kind of thing right now. About the way he sees, with his old-soul eyes.

It has been one of those weeks of wrestling with the angels. Of working out on the elliptical while the kids are napping, of listening to music and weeping, of speaking to a God who is more in love with us than I ever imagined. Praying one night for these little ones coming, and the next night for my boys and wondering if we are doing the right thing.

And then I see it. An open-roofed fortress around us, and within it, Trent and I holding up our boys, who in turn are holding up Danny and Sam, who are clasping the hands of God.

So we form this sort-of staircase to heaven.

I can't explain the love I feel for them: like the shepherd who risked the lives of his ninety-nine sheep so he could find the one (or two, in our case), and trusting, trusting, that God will watch out for the rest of the flock while we bring the others home.

I see the lights of our car as it pulls into the driveway. I call Aiden and Kasher to me—both of them in their pajamas, scrubbed and shiny, Kasher crawling to the edge of the stairs and me picking him up—and we all stand in the doorway of the house, the glow from the kitchen behind us, and I hope we look welcoming.

And slowly, out of the dark of the garage emerge two tiny little boys, the taller one holding the shorter one's hand. They both have backpacks and they look so small between the drifts of snow as they walk the path to our house. Sam is just one and a half and not talking yet, his face a beautiful heart shape like his mother's, and Danny is four and slim, his face longer. Both with rich brown eyes and Aiden says "Hi," in a sweet voice as they slowly make their way to us. I bend low when they arrive, look in their eyes, say, "We're so glad you're here. You can call me Auntie Em."

I peel their winter jackets from them, their faces too old for their bodies. We show them their beds. Sam in a playpen in the den; Kasher in a crib in the nursery, Danny on the top bunk in Aiden's room, and Aiden on the bottom.

The boys are very careful around each other. Aiden keeps laughing and awkwardly patting Danny while Kasher pulls on Sam's sleeve. I try to make them feel at home by talking too much, saying, "We're so glad you're here to visit us! Aiden's excited to have you share his bunk bed, Danny. And Sam, I have a duck stuffy for you—it's in your bed. And we bought new blankets!"

We have a snack upstairs at the kids' table, yogurt and homemade cookies and then I go through the bag of clothes they've come with—mismatched pajama tops and bottoms, a few pairs of underwear for Danny, a couple of diapers for Sam. No socks.

We put them in their pajamas, brush four boys' teeth, say prayers and sing "Jesus Loves Me" beside each of their beds and hold them close so they won't feel alone.

And when Aiden has finally stopped weeping into his pillow for all of the change, and Danny has stopped crying for missing his mommy, and I've nursed Kasher for the final time that night and put Sam back in his bed after he tries to climb out, Trent and I sit upstairs on the couch in the dark.

Side by side.

Waiting for Immanuel to come and save us.

In the coming days, I scrape bowls of porridge from Sam's lap and pull his hand from the toilet and give him countless time-outs for hitting or throwing temper tantrums.

I give Danny time-outs for lying and Aiden time-outs for not listening to Mommy because he is not sure what to do with two new brothers. And Kasher crawling around smiling at everyone and then falling down the stairs because someone forgot to close the gate.

And when that happens, I pick up my youngest, who's hysterical, hold him so very close, try to tuck him back inside me somehow and I run to the office and close the door and sob, my whole body shaking.

"I can't do this," I tell God. "I'm wrecking my own children by taking on more. I can't do this," and slowly I calm myself down and Kasher stops crying and I put on some music and the kids run circles around the coffee table, laughing.

Danny cries every night for his Mama, and we put on *Dora the Explorer* and hold him.

All of us just trying to survive.

Sunday mornings are a panic, feeding four little boys in their Thomas PJs and putting them on the potty and changing them into four wrinkled pairs of dress pants and four dress shirts.

And Danny saying he wants to be Justin Bieber because his daddy wants him to look cool.

I put my hands on his shoulders so I can see deep into his eyes and I say, "Honey, it doesn't matter what you look like or who you are, we love you, and Jesus loves you too."

And we stumble into the pew at church, a family of six with bed heads and penitent hearts.

We are a full house, and there are toys and boots and mud and soup-stains, and sparing the guinea pig from sticky hands and rising countless times in the night when all of them get sick, which is all of the time, and trying to be like Jesus when we've had no sleep.

And every once in a while Trent and I look at each other across a mess of tousled heads and we see the person we want to be: the one hiding beneath the grime of the day-to-day, the one that weeps for all the children who have no one.

"I love you," we say, tired, to the other. Tucking under an afghan at the end of a day and watching our usual show with our chips and salsa, interrupted always by someone calling from bed needing a glass of water or another song.

It doesn't matter how many hugs I give Danny. How many times I tell him he is handsome in that white sweater—the one he wears to impress the neighbor girl even though he's only four—how many home-canned peaches I serve him or stories I read.

Come bedtime, it is his mother he needs, and all I can do is lie beside him and put my hand on his back and feel his heart pulling at his skin.

I know the first few months will be the hardest, like bringing home a newborn who feels like a stranger and then one day you wake up and he's become family.

And in the mornings they often feel like strangers, these boys, the tall one who cries when he loses the stick he buried in the snow outside, who hunts tigers in the woods and wants to be Superman when he grows up "so I can save my mommy," he tells me.

And Sam, who sticks his hands in everything and hits when he's mad, and laughs like the trees losing leaves in the fall, all colorful and free.

Come evening, though, they feel a bit like family.

We pray a lot with them, teaching Danny and Sam how to bow, and they do it over snacks and dessert and for their mommy too.

And I am relearning prayer, the way it is a kind of desperate plea when no one is listening and me, wading through trucks and crayons and dishes needing to be put away and the boys half-dressed and fighting over something and I look out the window and see a bird in flight.

And that bird becomes my peace. The way it rides the wind.

And as I lie beside Danny in the dark, so he won't feel scared, I recall how the boys couldn't stop eating pancakes and strawberries that night, how they crowded around Trent after bathtime for a

Bible story, ages four, two, one, and six months, all in Trent's lap, and it becomes my prayer. All of it.

That this boy will know the fullness of God's love, and that this love will become his Savior, here in the dark.

And one day, one week after they arrive, I am doing crafts with the boys, painstakingly gluing Danny's hundredth fuzzy ball to his creation, wondering why God has asked me to do this, a woman like me who has big ambitions and very little patience, when Danny looks at me and he says, "Emily, you're doing a good job."

I am learning that being a woman is about giving until it hurts, and then receiving so much that my soul might break.

It's the ebb and flow of the ocean, the washing and being refilled, the constant movement of creation. Because we create with our words, with our hearts, with our minds, even when our wombs are empty. Even when she physically can't conceive, a woman is always birthing. Always in labor. Always loving, because there are people growing around us, and because of us. There are husbands. There are someone else's children. There are friends and guests and all of these require the gentle surrender of a woman's time and passion.

And in turn, the Lord turns and tells us, "Well done, my good and faithful servant."

Through the voice of a child.

II

Church

Then the singing enveloped me. It was furry and resonant, coming from everyone's very heart. There was no sense of performance or judgment, only that the music was breath and food.

Anne Lamott

February 2012

I was the girl who always swore in the van on the way home from church.

Polite swears under my breath, my father driving, and I swore because I hated wearing pantyhose in the front row listening to a sermon by a dad I didn't know, about a God I didn't want to know.

And Mum would wash out my mouth with a bar of Ivory soap, like on the day I said "friggin" because I'd seen it spray painted on the wall of an abandoned building.

I felt like that abandoned building.

Like I was busy trying to decorate my outside but inside it was empty.

"That's where Jesus died," Danny says one afternoon, pointing to the hole in the paper he's scribbled with markers. It looks like an orange and yellow explosion, like a daffodil torn apart. "That's where it's all empty and gone."

He colors pictures for me during quiet time—the rest of the boys asleep and me typing furiously in the living room, with large mugs of coffee and bowls of chocolate chips to keep me awake. And Danny colors in the office. Paper and markers spread around him, and it's picture after picture, and he shows them all to me—some for his mommy, some for his daddy, and some for me. I hang mine up on the fridge with magnets and when Danny's mad at me he takes them down and says he's going to give them all to his mom.

"It's beautiful, sweetie," I tell Danny. He keeps looking at me after I say it, then looks down at his picture and back to me like he can't believe it.

I take his shoulders, again, making sure to see him. "You're such a good artist, Danny. I'm so proud of you."

And he smiles, his crooked teeth showing, and he runs back to the room to make me another drawing.

I am spreading strawberry jam on four pieces of toast, daylight breaking over the dirty dishes in my sink.

Easter has come and gone and left overstuffed stomachs and an empty tomb. My agent has called to let me know she's found a publisher for my eating disorder book. I have also received another book contract, and I have four boys in my house and no time.

I know the contracts have come because I've said yes to God. Because I took in his children. But I don't even have space in which to pray, let alone write, and my eyebrows are sparse because when I get anxious I pluck them.

"Remember two students will be coming over during lunch hour today to help you with the kids," Trent says, slipping into his shoes and grabbing his school bag, and I am suddenly crying into the toast.

"Will I ever get my old life back?" I whisper. My voice left yesterday, and all I have is a scratchy sound.

My pajamas are stained with jam.

"I just miss . . ." I say, and Trent nods.

"I know."

It had been so easy, before this. We'd found our place, as mother and father and two boys. We'd had laps and arms for both of them, and now we have no laps, no arms.

Today I am supposed to speak to the ladies at our church's midweek coffee break. I'm supposed to share about my anorexia journey, but I have no voice.

It's how I felt when I was young.

I tried out for the school choir when the doctor said I should be admitted into school at grade five. He said maybe I was lonely, maybe that's why I wasn't eating. So I walked to school with my red backpack and my curled-up bangs, and I tried out for the choir, but they said my voice was too quiet. They couldn't hear me.

So I quietly dropped my sandwich into the garbage and decided to let my eating disorder do the talking.

And I am looking for more than just jam in the fridge.

I am searching for faith and finding nothing but linens in the tomb.

Trent has come upstairs, is standing behind me now, and I grab his sleeve. "Can I have a hug?" I ask.

He folds me. Like I am paper.

"Always and forever," he says.

He hears me. Even though he calls me "Mumbles," he hears me.

"As Christians, we are meant to be not less human than other people, but more human, just as Jesus of Nazareth was more human," writes Madeleine L'Engle in *Walking on Water*.

I feel utterly human. I have never felt more human. *Humus*—Latin for earth, or ground.

And I need to be held in a way that gives me permission to be dust.

My voice shows up later that morning while I am speaking to a roomful of ladies in the church hall. Ladies from the Reformed Church, Dutch ladies with strong jaws and fierce eyes and curled steel hair, and many young ones with babies in car seats and they're rocking them while they listen; some children balanced on their mothers' laps and I'm stopping every few minutes to drink water while I talk, but they're listening. To my story of anorexia, to my fight with food, and for once I feel heard by the church.

We attend a large church here in the hamlet and I'm a bit of an outsider with my tattoos and piercings. I used to fear coffee time between services, because I don't wear dresses and I'm not from around here and there are tight circles of people who know each other. I'm grateful to have children to hide behind. But when they run off, I'm left standing in my thrift-store jeans trying to look like I have a place I belong.

I am stuck in that schoolgirl's body, the one who was chased around the playground, the one teased for being homeschooled and eating weird sandwiches and laughing too much.

And then we take in two more boys and I'm standing there before the church, a woman who's had no sleep and has yelled at her husband too many times that week and I no longer see competition. I no longer see cliques. I see mothers and grandmothers and wives and daughters with arms to help me. Because I need church desperately.

We've survived a couple of months with four boys ages four and under and I am threadbare. Tissue falling from one pocket and spit up on my shoes, a rip in my nylons and these women have arms to fall into. Hands to hold me up and I begin making phone calls the next day.

I call my neighbors—elderly women who say they'd love to come and take shifts. "Thank you," I gasp. "It's just until we figure out a long-term solution."

And so it happens that the church comes to live with us too.

Annie comes on Tuesdays, Grandma Lottie on Wednesdays, Miss Layla on Thursdays, to help me dress the boys and to read to them. The boys go swimming with Auntie Susan, feed chickens with Sally, make couch forts with Sara, color with Jeni, and play trains with April.

Other women come in the evenings when Trent is coaching and they help me bathe the kids and put them to bed, and I even have a friend who folds my laundry.

And every Sunday we walk down the road to church, and Danny and Sam see the women sitting there, in the pews. Their spiritual mothers, my church sisters.

"Why do you have so many neighbors?" Danny says. "My mommy doesn't have any."

My heart fissures like the shell of an egg.

"Because people here love each other, I guess," I say, swallowing. "And they love God."

One night after Trent and I pray together on our pillows, he turns to me. "I'm scared I'll never love them like they're my own," Trent says.

I think of him on all fours that afternoon after school, giving horsey rides to Sam and Danny and Aiden and Kasher. I think of him reading the Bible story of David and Goliath to them on the couch, praying with them—all bowed over and small with him—brushing their teeth and singing "Jesus Loves Me." I think of him throwing them into the snow and chasing them like a lion and putting them on his lap as he snowblows the driveway.

"But you already do," I tell him.

Speaking on what it's like to have four kids, comedian Jim Gaffigan says, "Just pretend that you're drowning; then, someone hands you a baby."

A typical day is Aiden and Danny stripping five times and jumping in mud and Sam peeing in the potty then dumping the pee on the floor and Kasher trying to crawl out of the Bumbo and onto the counter, and every once in a while, me emerging and gulping air, like when Danny hands me a bouquet of dandelions or Aiden asks to snuggle, and then it's waves of laundry and wet beds and fighting over toys and tearing pages out of library books.

So we hire a nanny. Because the boys need consistency and the church ladies are getting tired and I am too, of having different women always in my house. We hire a local girl with a sweet spirit and gentle hands who loves reading to kids and sewing and cooking. She introduces me to organic loose leaf teas with names like Banana Bread and Blueberry Pie, and plays the keyboard and makes us homemade noodles from scratch.

And Danny is teaching Aiden how to pull on his socks and Sam is giving Kasher kisses, and Christ is in our house.

"What does Jesus sound like?" Danny asks.

He is learning how to listen to God. I tell him prayer is about God speaking to us, and us speaking to him, and he keeps lamenting that he hasn't heard from Jesus yet.

And I say, "Remember that hug Auntie Susan gave you that made you feel warm and happy? That was Jesus. And remember how I told you I loved you today? That was Jesus, saying he loves you. Because Jesus lives inside of us."

I say this and then close his bedroom door and my eyes are scratchy because it has been thirty-one years and I still don't know when I am actually hearing God and when it is just my desperate heart making up stories. And it has been a long time since my house was quiet enough to hear anything except four little boys.

We make it to church, again, on a Sunday when I've forgotten to put on my makeup and everyone can see where I've cried, the tears crusted on my skin, because Sunday mornings are like that.

Me in the shower, feeling the hot water down my back and then four boys, knocking on the door. Because heaven forbid I have a shower without them.

"Just five minutes!" I beg, and Trent enters, tells me I actually literally only have five minutes before church is going to start and should he just take them without me, then?

I shake my head through the water, put a hand on the glass to hold myself up. "I'm coming," I say hoarsely. Because I want to go. I want to meet Jesus.

I want to meet him in the songs, in the sermon, in the farmers' faces around me.

Jesus has always been safe because he healed the sick, he hung out with sinners, and died for me, but his Father allowed so many to be killed and hurt in the Old Testament and had such hard rules. I don't know how they are the same God and so I speak to Jesus as much as possible but I know, deep down, I need more.

And the older I get, and the more of a mother I become, the greater I understand why Dad shut the office door and lost himself on the computer for hours at a time and didn't come home from church until late, because being unable to fix your children is difficult.

But that little girl still cries. The one inside me, the one who squints when she smiles and wraps her fingers around her wrists.

The same girl who was asked to speak with her dad just one year ago at a conference, pregnant with Kasher. We were asked to talk about our healing journey through anorexia, and then, the morning of our talk, Dad said something about the calories in the food at breakfast. I just shoved back my breakfast chair and walked away, for him not remembering that I used to be anorexic, that I used to count calories like I counted my ribs, and I did not want to go up on that stage and share about our journey through anorexia together.

But first, there was worship. Two hundred men and women and teens in one room, singing songs to God. I stood in the back with Mum and Dad and I closed my eyes and I saw heaven open. And Jesus was standing there, and I was a little girl running toward him. I wore a white dress and he picked me up, and he swung me around, and he told me over and over how beautiful I was. "Your ankles are beautiful, your legs are beautiful, your waist and your arms and your neck are beautiful, and I love you, Emily Theresa Wierenga."

I didn't want him to let me go but the song stopped and I opened my eyes, and then the next song started and I closed them again. And in my mind, I was back in heaven. And I was still a little girl in a white dress. But I was hiding behind a tree, not wanting to disturb Jesus, because he's the Creator of the universe. And I'm me.

And I was the same girl who stood outside her father's closed office door knocking, wondering if he would have time for her but not wanting to disturb him.

And then I heard it. Jesus's voice, calling for me.

He was searching in bushes, behind trees, looking everywhere.

Jesus Christ, the Creator of the universe, was looking for me.

And I knew, in that moment, that I was loved. I was wanted, not for any reason other than the fact that I was created. And I found the courage to forgive my dad, all over again, and to see him for the broken man he was who tried to love and who was willing to stand up on that stage with me and share his story of watching his daughter starve herself.

And afterward, we sang a song together, me playing the guitar, my father's beautiful tenor rising with my alto. We sounded good together.

It's Sunday, now. I step out of the shower, find a pair of wrinkled dress pants, a necklace and a shirt, and the boys are all in their white church shirts and little dress pants, waiting at the door.

And we go to church and I hand out juice boxes and granola bars to the boys lined up in the pew, and then I take Trent's hand.

And in front of me is a little girl with long blonde hair and a white dress. She's sitting beside her grandma, but when she begins to cry in the middle of the service her grandfather takes her into his arms. He's a big burly man who barely fits in the seat, but he looks down at her with such tenderness, as she leans her head against his chest. And I begin to sob, quietly.

12

Mum

A mother's body remembers her babies—the folds of soft flesh, the softly furred scalp against her nose. Each child has its own entreaties to body and soul.

Barbara Kingsolver

March 2012

I'm missing Mum this morning, as spring sings through the windows.

Trent has taken the boys to Oma's.

"It's my gift to you," he says, pulling on a light jacket. The snow has just melted here in Canada. There is frost in the air, but crocuses are rising bold and the robins nesting.

I sip my coffee and it's hot—I haven't had a hot coffee in months—and I'm writing a letter to Mum.

Growing up, I saw her bending worn over piles of bread dough, over the sink doing dishes for six people, over the washing machine and then stretching up to the clothesline and again, to take them all down, the pins in her mouth, the sheets and shirts smelling like the wind. Rising and falling, like a loom of life, weaving in and out across the strands of time.

In the evenings she folded that laundry, she planned home-school lessons and mended our clothes, because despite working overtime ministers don't make much and even the milk had to be mixed, from skim milk powder. Nothing was easy. There was no rest.

One day a month she'd ask Dad to watch us so she could go to the thrift store and buy us clothes, and sometimes she bought herself a shirt, but never anything new. And the clothes she did wear were billowy and long because even though her name, Yvonne, means "beautiful girl," she never knew she was.

I pause, pen to my lip, the house so empty and quiet I can hear a robin in the tree outside our back porch. Beneath the porch is a nest the boys have been watching daily, crouched low, bums in the air, squealing over the blue eggs cracking, the hairless little birds huddled close, the growing of fuzz and feathers.

I wish Mum lived closer than forty hours away, could see how my own babies are recklessly growing. All four of them, and she hasn't even met the latest two. The ones whose mother is coming later today to spend the afternoon with us. We're taking her to the sand hills outside of Vega, where the earth rolls red and the boys tumble and everything is a loud chorus of hallelujah. It's so beautiful there, and I long for Mum to see it. She could walk the trails with me because she's strong enough now. The tumor is gone, the doctors say, and I thought I was going to lose her.

Dad thought so too. That's why he took a photo of the double rainbow on a day shortly after Mum's second brain surgery. It was God telling him everything was going to be okay, and I didn't know. I didn't know how much he loved her until she nearly died.

We got a duckling, recently, with the kids. Our nanny brought it home because she's lovely like that, in a way that wears home-sewn skirts and sings. And brings a brand-new duckling into our home, all fuzzy and yellow and tucked in the folds of her jacket.

It lived for three days, and at first it was strong. It huddled in the boys' hands and we fed it milk and grass in a cage and let it toddle across the carpet with its webbed feet. But then one day it couldn't move its neck. Its neck just bent, and its eyes looking up at us sad. I'm not sure if one of the boys handled it too roughly, but they're so young they handle everything roughly. And the duck, its neck just hung broken until its eyes closed and it died.

We carried it out to the back lawn, to the apple tree we had planted in the fall, and we dug a hole for it in the ground, still hard from winter. Its yellow body so soft with fuzz, its head folded over its chest, and the boys, so very gentle with it, laying it in a bed of straw there in the ground.

The apple tree with its tender white blossoms, as we covered up the duck and the boys and I held hands for just a minute before they ran off to play and I wept my way into the house.

I don't do well with death. I was the girl who turned anorexic after her Grandma Ermenie died. The woman who used to play cards with me and taught me how to knit while we watched TV in her overheated apartment. I was the girl who *couldn't* cry at her Nanny's funeral after Mum found her dead in the bathtub, slit red from the razor.

I rise, rinse my coffee mug in the sink. Run my fingers through my short bob. If only I had been there for Mum when she first got sick. I wish it hadn't taken me so long to go home.

I was angry at her for reasons that weren't her fault. I understand now, how easy it is to yell at your children. How tiring this whole parenting thing is. How very much depends on God and how very little depends on us.

I read Mum's journals when she was asleep for days with brain cancer, the journals Dad pulled from the closet, and I traced her tiny handwriting, that blue felt script, and penmanship is a lost art these days.

While she slept in that dark quiet room with Dad's makeshift curtain across the window, I sat in a chair by her bed and read her words, because she felt more alive then. I was so scared I was going to lose her there beneath the sheets. Her face so pasty white and not eating or walking or talking for days, Dad and I just changing her and washing her blankets and turning her over so she wouldn't get bed sores.

But when she awoke, she'd smile at me and say, "Hello, Beautiful," and tell me she'd been praying.

Now that her tumor is gone, Mum doesn't sleep past three or four in the morning. She sits in bed in her flannel nightgown and prays for all four of her children, and it's a mother's prayers that bring the world to its knees.

Her photo is on my bedside table. A black-and-white of Nanny holding Mum. Nanny is in her late twenties, her wavy brown hair and teardrop face, her small smile as she holds a toddler in a frilly dress she no doubt sewed, and Mum is looking at the camera curiously as if wondering what she should do. If she should be happy.

I keep it there at my bedside, beside my stack of twenty books and my Bible, to remember forgiveness. The way it found me on a run three years ago when I was caring for Mum. And to remember my legacy.

Nanny's body was scarred from a bone disease she had as a little girl and Granddad would try to tell her she was beautiful, but she'd just shrug lower in her cardigan and do another oil painting, knit another sweater, try her hand at calligraphy, and eventually divorce her husband and move from England to Canada to live beside my Mum in a one-story flat.

My sisters would take turns bringing Nanny her mail, and she'd giggle with them, blow raspberries in their ears. And Mum would visit Nanny most afternoons for tea, and even though Nanny had never said "You're beautiful" or even "I love you" to Mum, she was invited over for meals and, at Christmas, did puzzles with us at the table. Nanny didn't believe in God, but she believed in art and beauty.

And then one June day when the lilacs were dropping purple, the sound of songbirds in the woods, Mum walked across the yard, past the chicken coop and the garage, down the path to Nanny's. The screen door open and the smell of cigarette smoke wafting, like incense, and classical music on the radio. Mum knocked and Nanny opened the door in her green cardigan and long black skirt.

She nodded at the sofa and Mum sat with her, told her about the new ministerial position Dad had been offered by a church in Southern Ontario—a full-time position, with a house, versus the part-time job he had now.

Nanny snuffed out her cig and drew in a shaky breath, coughed, then said, "Well, what will happen to me?"

Mum handed Nanny some brochures, glanced down at her hands. "We would have to find some form of assisted living in the same town—would this be okay?"

"No."

"What do you mean, Mum? Ernest has already accepted the position . . ."

Nanny stood up, pushed her shoulders back and walked a few steps into the kitchen, put the kettle on. Grabbed another cig, Bach's Fugue in D Minor on the stereo.

"I will be staying right here. I just moved from England; I'm not moving again. Now if you'll excuse me—please don't come and visit me again until Sunday," and she huffed her way into a seat at the kitchen table by stacks of cards and letters and Mum made her way to the door, paused.

"I love you," she said, without turning around, and then walked out into June's light and birds and the smell of lilacs.

My sister Meredith took Nanny her mail on Friday, and then on Sunday Mum walked across the yard again to have tea. Nanny's curtains were drawn. No classical music, no cigarette smoke, the door locked. Mum asked Dad to get the key, and they opened the house, letters and cards still piled on the table, and the door to the bathroom ajar. Mum walked slowly down the hallway to the bathroom, opened the door and stifled a scream. Nanny, dead in the bathtub, a razor in the water.

Mum crumbled, cried, then opened the living room curtains. Searched for a note among the cards and letters and there was none.

No note, just a woman who'd spent her life hiding behind sweaters, only to die baring it all.

Nanny never knew she was beautiful. Her dad never told her.

Mum didn't know she was beautiful. Nanny never told her.

I didn't know I was beautiful, because Mum never told me.

And three years after Nanny's suicide Mum contracted brain cancer.

Three years after that, I moved home to take care of Mum, and Mum started calling me Beautiful and it happens like this.

The shame, it just sort of lifts, like a red balloon, when we open up our hearts and let each other in.

I'm downstairs now, in my bedroom, finding clothes in the laundry basket, folded and waiting to be put away, and beside Nanny's photo is a recent family one, and in it Mum is laughing. I pick it up, the sunlight shining through our basement window, and I brush off the dust.

Mum is stunning, really, with those bright blue eyes and her pink cheeks, with her new brown hair that's covered up the scalp they cut away twice, to steal her brain. The right frontal lobe, and it's grown in so soft like new skin, this hair. And she's always smiling.

"It's because of Jesus," she says. "He gave me my smile, back in university, when I met him."

Mum praises better than anyone I know.

Even when she was sick with cancer and couldn't walk, if the worship music came on she'd know every word. And she'd dance. Raise her shaky hands and sway from side to side.

I'm not sure if Mum even knew I was pregnant with Aiden.

She would sit in her blue chair and stare at her Christmas amaryllis, which never flowered, and most days she'd sleep.

And one day I begged God to take her to heaven because it's hard to believe in anything good when your father is crying.

Eight years of tumor, and now it's gone. The doctors bewildered and God in his glory, and Mum, holding her grandbabies.

When I saw her after Christmas at my sister's house in Calgary, she said, "I love you, Aiden," as she pulled him to her lap, and they watched *Curious George* together. And they laughed at the same parts.

And she sang Kasher to sleep when no one else could get him quiet. Only taking a break when she had to go to the bathroom—and then she held my baby some more. And when I next looked in on them both, Mum was curled around him on the bed, both of them asleep.

Two years ago she couldn't even hold a cup of coffee without spilling it, now she's rocking my babies. And this Christmas, the amaryllis finally bloomed.

And sometimes when I can't rest—my faith, wandering around like a lost child—I think of Mum holding Kasher in the dark. I think of the way she wouldn't let go, even when he kept crying.

The boys will be here soon and my coffee is gone but spring is still singing. I'm going to hug them so tightly and tell them how much I missed them, because one day they'll be gone, with their own mailboxes and front porches.

Aiden's stretching so tall for only two years old and he clings to Danny, but he cries a lot too because it's all so new to him. Not even a year ago I bore him a brother and now he has three, but most of the time he runs around with underwear on his head screaming and throwing balls and ramming into walls.

I can hear them, now, running toward the house, all eight feet, four pairs of boots and four voices.

"I love you biggest," I say, bending low and hugging them at the door.

Rising, then, to kiss Trent.

Bending, rising, weaving life across the loom of the universe.

13

Raising Boys

When Jack Burns needed to hold his mother's hand, his fingers could see in the dark.

John Irving

June 2012

Trent is frying fish and the counter is covered in flour. Dandelions sit in a vase on my windowsill, the ones Danny brings me every day. It's five o'clock and we're nearing summer, the length of the day yawning around us.

Aiden is standing on a chair beside his dad. I am cleaning windows in the living room, and Danny and Sam are running around dressed as Batman and Robin. Kasher is chewing on a rubber toy and there's kids' music on.

I hear Aiden, even as Trent's chopping up potatoes from last year's garden crop; he's slicing them lengthwise for fries, and he'll lay them in olive oil on a stone pan and sprinkle cumin and garlic salt and chili pepper on, the fish frying and the air humming like a happy soul.

"When I grow up, I be like Daddy," says Aiden. "Big and strong and making nice suppers."

I look at Trent then, who raises his head and I see the surprise in his eyes. "Thank you, Aiden—how about chopping firewood? Do you want to chop firewood like me? Maybe fix bikes like me or rototill the garden?"

Aiden's hair is long, and he brushes it aside, this two-and-a-half-year-old with the deep eyes. "No," he says. "Just make nice suppers."

Trent laughs.

Soon we're sitting around the table, two boys in booster seats, one in a high chair, their food cut up and Danny beside me. The fish and fries on our plates, and I clasp Trent's hand as he prays, his voice covering the food, the family. "Thank you, Lord, for this food, for all that you give us. Help us to serve you. Amen."

The boys' voices exclaim "Amen!" and even as we eat, the clamor of children and forks and spoons dropping and Kasher pounding on the table with his tiny fists and Aiden and Danny singing at the top of their lungs, I remember the image God gave me as I was working out one night, months earlier. Me on the elliptical, replaying a friend's fears that we would wreck our own sons by taking on more.

I want to be a good mom. But I also want to be a good follower of Jesus, and I remember the open-roofed fortress, the picture God gave me of us forming a staircase for the boys to climb to heaven, and Trent at the bottom, supporting us all.

After the fish and fries, Trent pulls out the *Jesus Storybook Bible* and we read, the boys who've finished their plates piled on his lap. And then it's bath time and I clean up while Trent runs the water, Aiden's words in my ears. "Daddy, when I grow up I want to be like you," and I wouldn't know how to raise boys if it weren't for Trent.

I could nurture them and inspire manners, I could teach them ABCs and 123s, but when it comes to showing them how to live, boys ultimately need a man.

But I am his helper.

They're fighting in the bath, and Trent is on his computer. He looks at me wearily across the hall, and I nod. "I'll go," I say, because we pass the baton this way. And I go in and I use my stern mother voice. "Hey! What's going on?" And there are toys thrown across the floor and water and Kasher is crying.

Danny's not looking at me, and Sam is pointing at Danny and Aiden is putting a hand on Kasher's shoulder. "You okay?" he says.

It's hard to be mom to all of them in these moments. It's hard not to pick up Kasher and punish Danny just because I suspect he's guilty and my flesh and blood is crying. But I force myself to bend on my knees before them and look them in the eyes. Turn their faces, and kiss Kasher's and ask them for their stories. "What happened?" I say.

"I didn't do it," Danny says, and he picks up Hulk and starts playing. Sam points at Danny again, says "He lying," and Aiden's tossing foam letters into a bucket.

Kasher raises his chubby arms, and I breathe deep, pull my baby from the water, tell Danny he has five minutes to tell me the truth.

Wrap Kasher in one of the four towels I bought for the boys—all different colors, hanging on the rack—and take him to the couch. Hold him and kiss him, the red place by his eye where someone must have thrown a toy, and I pray.

I've never tried to love anyone as much as I try to love Danny and Sam and this isn't because I feel it. Most days I don't. But that's why the love is so real—because I try to live as though I do feel it. Some days I fail. But always, I try.

Because I want them to become men who try. I was reading about the *Titanic*, and 1,339 men died that night, but only 114 women and 56 boys and girls. And do you know why? Because men were not afraid to be men. They were not afraid to stand up and protect their loved ones.

And the manliest of those men that night was Rev. John Harper of Glasgow, Scotland. He cried out, "Let the women, children, and unsaved into the lifeboats." Then he kissed his only daughter, Nana, goodbye and placed her in the hands of one of the ship's officers aboard a lifeboat.

Soon, he found himself in water, and this is what an eyewitness, author Ned Ryun, describes as happening next:

> Concerned not with his life, but for the dying around him, Harper with his last breaths swam to the dying souls and cried out for them to be saved—"Believe on the Lord Jesus Christ and thou shalt be saved."
>
> As his strength began to ebb, Harper called out to a man clinging onto a piece of timber, "Are you saved?"
>
> "No," was the reply.
>
> A few moments later, Harper and the man came into contact again. "Are you saved yet?"
>
> "No," was again the reply.
>
> "Believe on the Lord Jesus Christ, and thou shalt be saved," Harper cried out one last time and with that, slipped beneath the waves.
>
> The young man clinging to the board was rescued and was later to testify that he had indeed been saved that night, not only by a rescuing ship, but by the words of John Harper.[1]

These boys we're raising, they'll be men one day, and how to teach them to care for one another, to protect their brothers, when they see fathers hurting mothers?

But for God.

Their true father, the One who died so the world might live, who rose so the world might know heaven.

I hear his voice saying, *These are my children—take care of them for me*, and I see him, like a shepherd, standing guard over all the world's young.

1. Moody Adams, *The Titanic's Last Hero* (West Columbia, SC: Olive Press, 1997) as quoted in "John Harper: True Hero on the Titanic," accessed February 17, 2015, http://www.blessedquietness.com/journal/housechu/harper.htm.

They have no one else, Jesus tells me, and so I breathe. Kiss Kasher who's trying to grab his toes, place him on the ground and let him roll, and I walk back into the bathroom.

Kneel down again on the blue rug that's soaked with water, and Danny's thin face and long lashes find me. "What happened?" I say again.

"I don't know," he says.

I shake my head. "Danny, I'm not going to punish you for telling the truth. But I will punish you for lying. Just tell me the truth, and then everything will be okay."

He looks slowly up at me, and I see the question in his face. *Why did you take me away from my mommy?*

This is about more than raising a boy; this is about saving a child, and I need to be tender, gentle, as I am with my seedlings when I transfer them into the ground.

"It was an accident," he says, now. I nod. "I was just playing and I threw it and it hit Kasher in the eye."

He cringes. I touch his bare shoulders. "Good job, Danny. I'm so proud of you for telling me the truth."

Sam laughs. Aiden says he wants to come out now, and I walk out of the bathroom, pass the baton to Trent, who rises from his computer chair and helps the boys clean up the bath toys, get into their pajamas.

And I take Kasher downstairs in the cool of evening, past the train table, into the nursery with its yellow walls and bright acrylic paintings. I lay him on the change table and my tears fall on my baby as I dress him.

Aiden and Danny are covered in melted popsicle, grape and orange, and they're riding bikes up and down the deck and laughing at the robins hopping across the lawn.

Aiden stops and looks at me, sitting on the front step in my flannels with my Bible. He's my oldest, and "It's a beautiful day,

Mommy," he says, because that's something he hears me say, whenever it's sunny.

And then he rides his bike some more and brakes in front of me, asks, "Mama, can I be a girl?"

I look up.

"No, son," I say. "God made you a boy. He has a special plan for you, as a boy. And one day you'll grow up to be a man."

Aiden looks at Danny, who's listening, then back to me. "Like Daddy?"

I nod. "Like Daddy, or Opa, or Grandpa."

His forehead wrinkles. "Okay. I boy?"

"Yes, Aiden, you're a boy."

And there is something resolute in the way he sits back on his bike and rides because he needed to know that.

That night, I'm leaning over his bunk, tucking Aiden in. "God has called you to be a leader," I whisper. He's clinging to his green bunny, running his fingers over the little bow on the bunny's collar. And I remember how God spoke over him when he was a newborn, said, *This is your tenderhearted leader.*

"A bleeder?" Aiden says.

I smooth back his hair and smile. "Yes. A man who will help people."

"Okay."

And isn't this what a true leader is? Someone who dies to himself, who bleeds for others?

But then there are boys who literally bleed. One afternoon I ask Danny to go to the dump with Trent and the boys, and he refuses. I tell him it's not a choice, so he gives himself a bloody nose, seeping red all across his white pillowcase.

It had been one of those gasping kinds of weeks, the kind in which I held myself together with multiple cups of coffee and pieces of dark chocolate and mental pats on the back. And lots of Scripture.

But there's no Bible verse that can quiet the ache of a little boy's heart, there's only a mother's arms and a father's handshake.

A parent is a little boy's gospel.

And I've prayed so many days that God would let us be the gospel for these boys and give me the words and the ways and we've cocooned them here, these past few months.

But I see the sorrow of the world crippling Danny.

"My heart is bleeding," he tells me one night. And the next morning, after he makes Sam cry, I shut the door and pull him close.

I try to make room for grace, to build it a cozy nest.

I hug him so tight both of us stop breathing, and it's in this shared space of sorrow that God enters.

I have no words, only arms, but *I'll offer them a hundred times a day just to let you know you're loved.*

14

Flood

You keep the promise anyway. That's what love is. Love is keeping the promise anyway.

John Green

July 2012

It is raining. It has been raining all day, and not the gentle warm kind of rain, which baptizes. No, this was metallic, like hundreds of tiny nails falling from the sky.

Mum is talking to me on the phone, her soft British voice pressed to my ear as I scrub dirty dishes. It is nearing the end of July. Sweet peas climb the fence outside and every time I walk past, carrying buckets of strawberries or raspberries to can into jam, I stop to smell them. Mum's nickname for me growing up was Sweet Pea, and they smell like jasmine, their pink and purple folds shivering in the rain.

We are leaving in five days for Young Life camp in the cracks of the Rocky Mountains, and Danny and Sam will be staying at their grandparents' in the city. It will just be us—my man and my two boys whom I miss desperately.

We are always with each other but never really. They are just out of reach, because the house is so crowded with children who need more than our family can give.

And I am trying to be patient but I only have two arms.

And I miss the smell of my own sons. The smell of earth and skin that I bore and nursed.

"It's my prayer for you," says Mum into my ear, now, the grease stuck hard and me, scrubbing. "I want you to be an overcomer."

The toilet downstairs is gurgling, and Trent has gone outside to check the sewer but can't see anything in the wet. So he returns and we put down the toilet lid, try to ignore it for the hubbub of boys and the packing for our trip. But after supper I go downstairs again, and something is starting to smell. Like fish.

All four boys are in the tub, the sound of splashing and singing and toys and bubbles.

"Me too," I tell Mum, phone pressed to my ear. "I want to be an overcomer too," and even saying that is a victory.

I drain the water and clean out the sink, and Trent washes the boys and all four of them wrapped in towels come running out of the bathroom into the living room where we turn on some music and they begin to run squealing around the coffee table.

"Watch me, watch me," Danny is saying, jumping from the couch to the floor in his brown skin and then Aiden and Kasher crawling, trying to climb and Sam jumping and skinning his knee. And soon it is bandages and kisses and finding clean pajamas out of the dryer and singing "Jesus Loves Me." Prayers and cups of water and night-lights on, and then quiet.

Except for the toilet, gurgling.

And that's when I say something to Trent. "Something's not right, hon—something stinks."

Back when Harvey owned pigs, and Trent was a young boy mucking out the stalls in his blue overalls, hauling wheelbarrows full of manure, he lost his sense of smell somewhere between the barn and the house and it never fully recovered. So he hasn't noticed the house smelling like an unflushed toilet, but when I say that he walks the hallway to the furnace room. And that's when his feet get wet. Because the carpet is soaking.

And he opens the door to the furnace room, and there is silence. Then, "Em, there's an inch of water covering this entire room. This is not good. This is not good at all."

Our house is flooding.

The hose had broken and while the boys sleep, Trent locates a water vacuum at the farm, his parents having left that day for vacation in Alaska. But it isn't enough; the walls and floor are drenched with sewage, smelling of feces and urine and all the bedrooms downstairs are soaked because we hadn't thought to open the furnace room earlier.

So then Trent borrows a sump pump, and we pump sewage water out of our house onto the lawn, and all the next day too.

And we tear up the carpet, which is drenched and reeking, and we move the bunk beds—the boys climbing across the wood frame—and yank up the underlay in every room. Move mattresses upstairs and it will be a slumber party, we decide, in the living room, the boys jumping on our queen-size.

At one point I nearly curl over and sob, thinking about leaving in a week and what if we can't? But there is too much to do and my boys need me too much, so I pull my spirit up by its bootstraps.

And I practice saying thank you to God while we roll up the carpet and dump it out on the lawn, while we towel up the floor and get rid of the furniture and toys and anything that has been resting on it.

And we call the insurance company. They are booked solid because houses everywhere have been flooding.

But I swallow and say thank you because our house is still standing. And all of our boys are safe and we still have mattresses to sleep on, and meanwhile Japan has just been rocked by a tsunami.

Thankfulness smells a lot like sweet peas.

So I make the boys some tomato soup from a can and put on *Curious George*. They lie stomach-down on the mattress and I go to the office, a bowl of chocolate raisins in my hand, the breakfast dishes still dirty on the table, the flood still downstairs.

And I sit, scrolling through Facebook.

A well-known writer has posted an interview with homemaker Martha Stewart, in which she talks with Stephanie Ruhle of Bloomberg Television.

Stephanie asks Martha what brands she trusts and who she thinks has good taste, and Martha says it's impossible to be too big. She says bloggers aren't experts because they aren't editors at *Vogue* magazine. Martha is confident and classy and calculated.

She is who I wanted to be when I was twenty-three.

Flying home from our honeymoon in the Maritimes, from weeks of hitchhiking and making love and sandcastles, and I was scribbling furiously on a napkin in that plane, trying to come up with menus for the next month. Because I'd suddenly realized I was a homemaker. And I didn't know what that meant. But I wanted to do it well.

I didn't know what it meant except for tired, because that's what my mum always was. Her making everything from scratch, and Trent didn't know but I'd slipped back into an eating disorder months before our wedding day beneath the trellis in my parents' backyard.

So here I was planning out menus for meals I wouldn't eat.

When the plane touched ground in Edmonton, the honeymoon ended. We rented a basement suite from friends and we didn't have any furniture except an old sunken couch we'd been given and a bed, so we bought a table and chairs from Value Village and some shelves and I sat on that depressed couch and mourned, because I wanted our house to be a beautiful place for my husband to come home to.

Soon afterward, we moved into our first house—a white duplex on a corner lot one block from an adult video store and a five-minute drive from the school Trent worked at for Young Life.

I filled every nook and cranny with fake flowers and wreaths and candles and I painted the walls. I painted the hallway and the kitchen and the bedrooms, and there were baskets holding slippers and it smelled like cinnamon and it looked like home.

But if Trent got dirt on the welcome mat I would burst into tears.

"Did you touch the lamp?" I said one night after a full day at the newspaper I edited, after driving girls around for Young Life and not eating. "Did you touch the lamp, Trent? Please answer me."

He stepped out of the office down the hall. "I may have—I don't remember; why?"

I threw up my hands. "Now something doesn't look right. I had the doily, and the lamp, and now it's crooked and thanks a lot. Just—thanks."

I stormed upstairs to the tiny attic where I painted on my easel, the one Trent had made me months earlier in the basement suite.

I turn now to a different clip online, of the friendliest neighbor, Mr. Rogers, who received a lifetime achievement award. He's not classy or put together, but he's warm. And he's touched so many lives. This is what he says in his acceptance speech: "So many people have helped me to come to this night. Some of you are here. Some are far away. Some are even in heaven. All of us have special ones who have loved us into being.

"Would you just take, along with me, ten seconds to think of the people who have helped you become who you are? Those who have cared about you and wanted what was best for you in life?"[1]

I want my home to be a place where I love people into being.

We're all like broken-down houses—no amount of paint or wallpaper can fill the holes.

And I'm learning it's okay to be broken like this. To eat chocolate raisins and scroll through Facebook like this while the flood rises. It's okay to not be as collected as a Pinterest mom who has

1. Fred Rogers Acceptance Speech – 1997," YouTube video, 3:12, uploaded by emmys, March 26, 2008, https://www.youtube.com/watch?v=Upm9LnuCBUM.

a chalkboard with tonight's menu on it, or a bouncy castle for a
birthday, or a string quartet for an anniversary.

It's okay to not always have my hair washed or the jar of cookies filled. It's okay to order takeout. A mother's greatest saving
grace is the number of a good Chinese restaurant. And it's okay.

So long as there is love.

But then Trent says something like, "Maybe we won't be able
to go." Maybe we won't be able to leave in five days for Young
Life camp.

He says it in the playground by the school because we are taking
a break from the smell of sewer, from the windows wide open and
the floor still sopping and little boys' soaking socks piled in a heap.

We both look like sponges dripping across the playground, rocks
in our sandals and our armpits stained with work.

My lengthening hair is shoved into an elastic, matted for not
washing, and my hands still smell like tuna even though I've
scrubbed hard, and my skin feels like salt.

Three boys between us hanging off bars and flying down slides
and Kasher's crawling on the ground, on the pebbles, trying to
eat them. There's a cloud that looks like a bowl of ice cream on a
blue tablecloth of sky, and all I want is that. A bowl of ice cream,
a novel, and a place to put up my feet.

"We might not be able to go," Trent's saying, even as I scoop
pebbles from Kasher's mouth, "because if insurance needs us to
stick around and the basement isn't cleaned out in time, well, yeah,
we'll just have to be around to fix it, that's all."

I feel the anger like it's a turtleneck and I can't breathe. I can't
stay. I need to leave, to the mountains, to a place that doesn't smell
of toilet, to a place without four boys in the upstairs of a house,
without a queen mattress in a living room, without meals to be
cooked and laundry to be done and groceries to be bought, and
"No!" I snap, a brittle twig, and Trent goes quiet. The boys turn

their heads, but I throw up my arms. "No, you can't say that. We have to go. We have to. We have to."

Kasher's looking up at me, his ruddy cheeks and hazel eyes and there's a rush of wind through leaves, and Aiden's whimpering, "Mommy?" from the teeter-totter with Danny.

All I can see is the wagon, the red plastic one with the wheels that whine on gravel and I grab Kasher, and he grabs my hair, and I put him in the wagon. "I'm going home," I say.

"Emily, you're acting like a baby," Trent says.

"I know, and I don't care," and I turn to leave because the tears are coming. Months of tears, vaulted from late nights of kissing foreheads and bringing glass after glass of water, from writing books in-between and weeding carrots and onions and coming up for air before heading into date night and laundry and dishes.

The vault, broken for all of Neerlandia to see as I walk the red wagon home, the plastic wheels whining on the stones, the houses a mad blur of walls and windows. Kasher sitting silently behind, sucking on his fingers. All I want is home. But our house isn't home right now, it's a wet mess of carpet and unpacked bags and bags of clothes, our furniture all stacked in the garage.

My friend is kneeling in her garden as I pass, bowed low over her flower garden, and I tap her shoulder and she turns. I blubber something about Trent and she takes me in her arms. She's a single mom and she hugs like a woman who's cried before.

"He loves you," she says. "He loves you, he loves you, he loves you."

Somehow this is what I need. I breathe in and out and my friend puts her hand on my shoulder. "It's hard to see sometimes, but I see it, Em," she says. "I see the way he looks at you. I want someone who looks at me like that."

I nod. "You deserve someone like that," I say.

I pick up the wagon handle, the whine of the wheels on the road and somehow, I find my way home.

Three bikes and a tricycle pull in; Trent's home with the boys, and I've got supper on the table. We're having sandwiches and potato chips tonight, because that's the kind of day it's been—not even carrot sticks—and I'm standing by the door when he comes in, because I want my hug to be the first thing he feels about our house.

I bury my face in his shirt—the washed-out Calgary Flames one with the exhausted neck-hole—and it smells like the earth after winter, fresh, soddy, moist. "I'm sorry," I say into the cotton.

"Me too," he says.

That evening we're in the basement for another round of cleaning, streaks of dirt on our faces and Aiden balancing in his bare feet on the rolls of carpet. Laughing, falling off, climbing back on. And this is all adventure for him.

And I'm watching him, realizing at some point I stopped being that girl who would bike to the park with Trent at midnight and make out on the grass. I stopped climbing new heights and facing my fears, because it was safer on the ground.

And I look at my son, see a boy who knows no fear.

And he is laughing.

We make it out in time, the basement scrubbed and drying and the insurance company promising to come as soon as they can. I picture our house fully restored by the time we return.

Danny and Sam go to visit their grandparents, and we drive to camp in the jagged cliffs of the Rockies, in the hidden valley of Princeton, British Columbia, where Young Life's resort, Rockridge, sits with 1,500 acres of trees and fields, buildings carved out of wood and glass, nestled against Inspiration Lake. Hundreds of kids arriving each summer from the ghettos of cities and schools to zip across the longest line in Canada, to water ski and wakeboard in the early mornings across the lake, to climb the Tower of Terror and hike the edge of the mountains, to be served in an expansive dining room with waiters and four-course meals, because Young Life's philosophy is to reach kids with the love of Jesus—at all costs. The onsite hotel so new it still has sawdust in the corners. We don't have to make our meals—we gather in the main hall, the one that smells of cedar and has beams that touch the sky and panes of glass that let in the fullness of God's glory.

Aiden sleeps in the bunk beds partitioned off from our room and Kasher sleeps in a playpen, and I drink espresso in the main living space by a brick fireplace. And I sit. Completely still, my arms empty of children, holding nothing but time.

Trent is there as head leader, which means he leads the leaders and has their backs and makes sure kids are in their cabins after hours, and there is one kid named James who really needs loving. The kind of kid so starved for attention his face is gaunt.

One afternoon I am reading in bed, the kids napping, and Trent bursts into the room and asks me to pray for James. They've lost him, in this place of mountain and sky.

James hadn't eaten in two days. He wanted to get back at his dad for sending him here. He wanted to hurt his parents who were going through a divorce, so he was smoking pot in the guts of the rocks and hiding behind shower curtains when Trent came looking for him. And he screamed and swore at Trent when he found him.

Then he ran away, Trent following him and talking into his walkie-talkie, and it felt like a manhunt. So Trent slowed down. He lost sight of James, and he prayed, and then he caught sight of a sliver of black jacket from behind a tree. He sat down and waited. James saw this, and eventually they began to talk.

Trent apologized for it seeming like a manhunt, for all of this, but they cared about him, he said. Then God told Trent to go and get James some pizza—at this point Trent didn't know James hadn't eaten in two days—and so he did, and they talked some more.

This went on for the next two days, this chasing and hiding and not wanting to be at camp and Trent praying and seeking James out. And then someone reported three iPhones missing, and cash. And James, the only suspect.

He said he didn't steal them, but then when he thought no one was watching he slipped out of the cabin and scaled the mountains. Trent and the other head leader followed behind. They stopped to pray and God led them to a pile of rocks and wood and grass and they dug beneath it; found a bag with three phones and the cash.

And James was sent home.

But before he goes, I make him a paper bag lunch and Trent and I tell him we care about him and that we wish he could stay.

Later that night, Trent comes into our room, holding a plate of nachos. "Emily, will you come have a snack with me, and let me tell you how much I love you?"

So we sit in the moonlight, in the kitchen of the lodge, the campers partying below. We eat nachos and he tells me how much he loves me. For praying for him this week. For loving James alongside him. For letting him sleep in after he'd been out late searching for the boy.

And all of the stress of the past month, of the two extra children and the flooding and the not having arms enough, it's like a hole we fall into, and we rest there, holding each other.

And then we go home.

Two weeks of mountains and fine dining and building sand-castles on the beach with my sons. Two weeks of zip-lining with Aiden and hiking in the early mornings before the Canadian sun blazed hot across the lake.

Two weeks, and we drive home to an overgrown garden—the squash strangling the peas and the corn, and the insurance company has come. Has set up industrial sized dehumidifiers and sawed off our drywall but the floors and stairs are still unfinished—just bare planks of plywood—and our mattress still upstairs.

It will be months before the company can return to do any kind of work, they tell Trent on the phone. Or they can send us $18,000 and we can do it ourselves.

So we do it ourselves.

And that night, after we've thrown our laundry in the wash and unpacked the mountains into the living room, "We're blessed, honey, we really are," I say.

But even as I say it, I am trying to believe it. Danny and Sam are coming back in a few days, and it is hard to know where to put everyone.

The next morning the living room curtain catches fire because it is too close to the lamp because everything is squished. And the house smells like fire and flood and "We're blessed," I whisper to myself.

And we are.

I see it in the limbs of my boys, in the food in our pantry, in the roof over our heads, but when Trent gets discouraged—because he is going to be the one rebuilding the walls and carpeting and painting—then I do too, and when I ask him not to get angry he becomes angrier.

He needs me to let him be.

Faith allows us to feel. It is the belief that we are not in control, and therefore heaven is not dependent on our good works, and therefore we can just be, some days.

And even though we only have half a house, it is enough.

My friend wrote me recently, on the back of a postcard,

I believe some basic things, like that God loves me, he's my father, he's caring for me, and he wants to give me good gifts. He knows better than I do what a "good gift" is. So when I pray, asking for a good thing, I know he's happy to hear it, happy to give me lavish blessings . . . but I know too, that the most lavish blessings are perhaps best learned in difficulty—and in that way, I see his care through good and bad circumstances since I trust that he is acting in my life and using all these things to pull me closer to himself.

I am learning to climb the piles of sewer-soaked carpet and displaced clothing and ruined toys.

I am learning to touch the face of God.

15

Plastic Flowers

Do not anticipate trouble, or worry about what may never happen. Keep in the sunlight.

Benjamin Franklin

December 2012

Danny and Aiden are getting ready for bed, with mismatched pajamas and socks and wet hair from the bath, and I turn on the lava lamp—their night-light. We sing "Jesus Loves Me" and "Silent Night," and Danny is climbing the ladder to his bunk when I hear him say, "God is pretend."

I suck in air and then let it out like I am having contractions, and I say very slowly, "Oh no, dear Danny, no, honey, he is so very real. I talk with God every day."

He pauses, one foot above the other on the ladder and I realize I am gripping the side of the bed for support because it feels like he's slapped my faith upside the head.

He is only four, I keep telling myself, and it is a work in progress.

"But I can't see him," he says in a whisper and I nod.

I envision a summer's day and us on the lawn with the kite.

"You can't see the wind, either, can you?" I say. He is on his bunk now, with his Spiderman blanket.

"No . . ."

"But you can see a kite, moving in the wind, can't you?"

"Yeah . . ."

"Well, when you see someone loving on somebody else, that's like the kite. And God is the wind."

He nods.

"But Satan lives in the dark," he says.

I am not sure how little boys' minds work.

"Yes, but God is bigger than Satan. And if he lives inside you, he makes everything light, because . . . he has superpowers."

"Does Satan have superpowers?"

"Yes. Only he uses them for evil."

"Can I have superpowers?"

"No, but you can have Jesus living inside of you, and Jesus has superpowers."

I turn back to Aiden, who's been lying quiet the whole time.

And then I hear Danny say, "Well, I want Jesus to live inside me."

I look up at him and let out air again, because they are the words every Christian mother lives to hear. "Pardon?"

He says it again: "I want Jesus to live inside me," and then I tell him to climb down the ladder, and "Me too," says Aiden, climbing out of bed, because they are a regular Tom Sawyer and Huckleberry Finn—doing everything together. "I want Jesus to live in me too."

So we sit there on the bedroom floor, and we pray to Jesus—a stumbling, faltering prayer like, "Dear Jesus, Thank you for dying for me. Thank you for rising again. I am sorry for my sins. Please forgive me and come in. Amen."

And then I tuck two sleepy little Christians back into bed with their green bunny and their stuffed frog, kiss their foreheads. And it's brighter in that room than I've ever seen it before.

It's early December now, and Danny is sleeping beside a bouquet of plastic flowers to give to his mom tomorrow when he sees her. The boys are going home for two weeks this time. Up until this point, they've only seen their mom once every few weekends.

I've talked with Ashley every week for the past six and she's found an affordable place, and her friend has given her a job. She's found a Christian school for Danny, which will provide assistance for her and food and clothing for him, and which will teach him how to pray and how to write his name, and she's found a daycare close to home for Sam, also covered by assistance. And angels are filling the skies. As the days close in, and we pack their bags—with children's Bibles and books and clothes people have given—I hold them on my lap and read stories, pray over them and cry in the shower.

For all of me not feeling like a mother to these boys, my body knows them as mine, because it responds to them now—to their cries, to their hurts, to their late-night screams from the nightmares and me rushing to hold and soothe and sing "God Is Bigger Than the Boogeyman."

"Are you ready?" I say to her on the phone the night before I'm supposed to meet her at Superstore, to do the exchange, and I'm counting out juice boxes and bags of goldfish and granola bars.

"I think so," she says quietly. "I went shopping today and bought a ton of organic stuff—vegetables and whole wheat bread, and I folded all of their clothes and made their beds." She begins to cry. "Seriously, Em, you have no idea how you saved me this year. Thank you. I don't know where I'd be if it wasn't for you."

I sit by the Christmas tree that night, watching the lights blink red and blue and yellow, the bottom branches heavy with ornaments because those are the ones the boys could reach.

We'd chosen a tree together on a Saturday with Marge—her cancer firmly in remission—and Harvey in the old blue and red truck, bumping across snowy back roads to the woods, and Oma had brought hot chocolate in a thermos. Sam and Kasher, huddled with Opa under a shaggy spruce on a blanket, drinking hot chocolate while Trent and I and Danny and Aiden found a pine.

We hauled it home and strung it up and popped corn, hung it round and there was Christmas on the stereo and pizza in the oven. The house smelled like evergreen and candy canes while Bing Crosby sang "I'm Dreaming of a White Christmas."

The tree is blinking and I'm holding a mug of tea on the couch, hearing a house full of children's dreams, and I'm sending wishes, lots of them, to Jesus—*Keep them safe, Lord. Keep them whole, Lord. Help us all, Lord. Amen.*

Superstore is crowded and the four boys are in a cart, Sam and Kasher in the front, their little legs sticking out with boots on the end and Danny and Aiden crouching in the back, and I grab four Santa hats in one aisle, stick them on the boys' heads, and take a picture.

Danny's eyes are bright and he's watching the entrance to the store, clutching plastic flowers and a picture for his mommy. Sam grins when he looks at me and he's come so far, I don't want to let him go. He came a raging little child with cold hands and no socks, temper tantrums and biting, and now he leans over and kisses Kasher on the cheek, and he reaches out to me with two hands, pulls me close, says, "I love you, Emily."

Danny has fought me this year because he doesn't know how much I love his mother. He doesn't know I did all of this for her. He thinks I stole them from her and yet, so long as his mother remains his heroine, it's okay. She is the one whose name needs to be heralded, not mine. Every mother needs grace like this. I would tell myself this, even as he gave himself bloody noses and kicked the wall with his feet.

When she arrives at the Superstore entrance, the boys run to her and she scoops them up, and I stand back and smile with my boys clinging to me. She turns, says, "Thank you," and I tell her we're still here for her. That we won't stop taking care of them, or her, and then we step back and watch them go, waving.

Our hands seeming so small in the air, fluttering, like autumn's forgotten leaves.

Aiden has nightmares now.

He wakes up in a cold scream, in his new bed—because we moved him to the top bunk when Danny went home, "Where Danny used to sleep?" Aiden said, touching the headboard tenderly—and we moved Kasher from the crib to the bottom bunk, so Aiden wouldn't be alone, and we nailed a plank to the edge of the bottom bed as a rail to keep Kasher from falling out.

Kasher lies splayed now across the bottom mattress—his little arms and legs outstretched and his cheeks red—and Aiden crying from the top, for the dark dreams.

We fight the dreams with music and prayer and lava lamps and turtle flashlights. We fight them with late-night tears and early morning snuggles.

And over and over, we remind our eldest son with the old-soul eyes that the monsters, while real, are already defeated. That evil died when Jesus was born, that David killed the giant named Goliath, that children everywhere can kill the enemy through bedtime prayers.

Aiden whispers, "Satan, go away, in Jesus's name. Amen." And I tell him the light is brighter in him than in any lava lamp.

And he turns on his turtle and shines moons and stars on the ceiling and we talk about how God knows them all by name, all those stars. We name them: Bob the Builder, Caillou, and Danny and Sam and Aiden and Kasher, because it's hard to be afraid in the face of the familiar.

But then I walk upstairs and pour myself a glass of wine and sit in my chair, and I can't even check the news for the fear. I can only check my email, and that just barely, because when I watch the news, or read horrible stories, anxiety makes my spirit tremble.

It's why I went on mild antidepressants when Kasher was born. All of a sudden, two babies made the world with all of its pedophiles and nuclear weapons too much.

Worry robs a lot of women. Anxiety riddles us useless because we're suddenly responsible for these little lives and we can't even take care of our own.

I set my wine down carefully, and I cry carefully too, into my palms, because everything has to be controlled. A counselor told me recently that it's not that I'm a control freak. It's that my past was so unpredictable, my growing-up years so chaotic, and because I had no say over where we lived or what I wore, for so long, I am now desperate for order. I like my kitchen neat, I like my living room vacuumed at the end of the day, I like the toys where they belong, and I like quiet.

A week later, Trent and I go snowboarding in Jasper during Christmas break, the boys at Oma's, and on the way home we talk about New Year's resolutions.

"What do you hope for me?" he says, and I look at him.

"I hope that you'll always enjoy your job."

He nods. "And for you, I wish that you would stop worrying," he says. "That you wouldn't be so anxious, and that you'd take one day at a time." Then he breaks into song, like he sometimes does, "Because the Lord your God is with you!"

The Lord our God is with us. We just need to utter the trembling whisper, "In Jesus's name," and he will come. His light shining brighter than any lava lamp.

The stars all twinkling and known by name.

PART 4

Woman

We are women, and my plea is, let me be a woman, holy through and through.

Elisabeth Elliot

16

Stillborn Faith

I talk to God but the sky is empty.

Sylvia Plath

December 2012

And then it's gone.

The faith you claimed to have since you were eight and your father baptized you in the United Church in the name of the Father, the Son, and the Holy Spirit, the faith you temporarily lost in Vancouver when you were standing outside a Hindu temple in awe of the worshipers' reverence. The faith that saved you from anorexia when you were thirteen, which saved your mum from brain cancer when you were twenty-eight.

Like something as flimsy as one of the Kleenexes littering the floor where you sit, because the belief you had that God actually cares about you, that he's seen the sacrifices you made the whole past year, all that is gone.

I'm preparing an editor for you, I heard God say in the shower in November.

His name is John, I heard him say, and at the time, an editor named John was courting my manuscript—a novel I'd written called *Broken Bread*, and I laughed because I longed for a publisher to call home. A publisher that would be my family. Both of my books, to date, had been printed by separate publishers—small, one of them secular, and it was my dream to have a house believe in my work.

This whisper of *John* was God saying he'd seen the sacrifice Trent and I had made. And I clung to that voice, even as the editorial board approved the novel and sent it on to the publishing board.

But now I am sitting in my office chair, staring at the screen, Trent downstairs with our boys and outside our red van, hood dented where I hit a deer early that morning.

And I sit here, at home, staring at an email, quietly reading the Times New Roman font as though the words were expected. The words saying the publishing board had rejected the manuscript in the eleventh hour, and my agent is so sorry—she's been trying to call me all day, but I've been gone.

Outside it is grey. Snow on the ground and the sky a gaping kind of mouth.

And right after that email I open another that says one of the families I wrote about in the first edition of my eating disorder book, *Chasing Silhouettes*, was considering suing me because I'd forgotten to change their names in their story.

And I quietly close the black laptop and the white office door, lie down on the spare bed in the office—the one I've made up for Danny for when he stays overnight—pull the soft patchwork quilt my friend sewed for our wedding up to my chin and my chest just kind of opens up, releases a swarm of sobs like they are crows, like something has just died—and it has. My hope, it just lies shriveled on the floor and the birds attack it ferociously.

138

Trent is stoking the fire—I can hear the woodstove door open, aching on its hinges, and the air smells like smoke. Ashley will be arriving soon with the boys for their monthly visit and I need to start supper and I can't move. I pull my knees to my chin and hold myself like the baby I long for.

The other day I wanted to buy a pink snowsuit, because last spring, right after taking Danny and Sam in, Trent and I had both had the same dream of a little girl.

Trent saw her while biking past the home and farm center; she appeared out of nowhere—a picture of our daughter, in his mind. He said nothing to me about it, and then I went on a run that afternoon, past the very same center, and I saw her too: walking down the hall of our house, the one lined with photos, humming to herself. She wore a little white dress, and she had chubby cheeks and eyes like her father—dark brown with thick black lashes and her hair was brown and in pigtails. Her brothers wrestling in the living room but when she rounded the corner they ran to her and picked her up and twirled her because they loved her.

And the crib stands empty.

I am sobbing on the bed.

"What more do you want?" I cry to God. "I've given you everything, and you keep taking things from me."

I don't have anything else to give. I've spent every minute of the past year loving someone. I've spent every minute doing laundry, breaking up fights, and reading the same *Thomas the Train* story over and over. I've spent it baking bread and cookies and driving the boys to the city, and home, and praying for their mother and feeling paralyzed every morning for all the hard work that lies ahead. For all of the needs four little boys possess and the words and energy I don't have.

I've loved so hard my heart is like an old dishcloth.

And now, these emails. It was my fault for not remembering to change that family's name. It was a horrendous flaw on my part, forgotten in the three years it took to publish the book, and over the coming months we'll recall the thousands of books on shelves across the country and I'll rewrite that chapter, using a different family—and this time, remembering to use pseudonyms—and we'll do a second printing of the book, and I won't see a dime from sales for a long time due to the cost of it all.

My skin and the quilt are damp. The quilt smells like cotton and laundry detergent, and suddenly I ache for my Mum.

Her hands smoothing back my hair and saying everything is going to be all right.

But Mum is forty hours away and it's Trent who opens the door, and I don't want him to see me this way. Because then he'll know something is wrong, and I never make money with my writing and I don't want Trent to stop believing God's voice and I don't want to see that look cross his face: the one of deep, pained love masking concerned disappointment.

But he's here, anyway, and I can't breathe.

Trent pauses, closes the door behind him; he comes, kneels by the bed, and I keep shaking my head. "I didn't get it," I squeeze out. "They said no." Because he knows about the shower and God saying *John* and that I've been waiting all day to hear the news.

He just takes my hand. "Oh Emily, I'm so sorry."

And I remember losing her. Our first child. The cramps, the blood, how I'd sat with my legs tight together on the couch—the couch we'd found on the side of the road because Trent was substitute teaching and I was freelancing.

How Trent had come in from playing squash, his face flushed, and he'd seen me sitting there. I was supposed to be at a launch party at the local bookstore for my first book, but I'd called my sister. "I'm sick," I'd whispered. "Can you go for me?"

She hadn't asked any questions. I hadn't had any answers.

And Trent had entered our living room with its crimson walls and he'd smelled like sweat and dandelions.

He'd stopped short, asked what was wrong—had reached out and I'd said, "Don't touch me! You might hurt the baby," and he'd said it then too.

"Oh Emily, I'm so sorry."

Because a book is like a baby, a kind of giving birth, and there's an advent of sorts—a holy waiting—and you anticipate, even as you grow. Burgeoning with life and words. But when the baby is stillborn, or miscarried, your faith is too.

Stillborn faith.

And I hold my legs tight and sob, Trent saying he'll get supper and take care of the boys and "Don't get up," he says, "just rest."

17

Skinny

We have to get rid of this notion—"Am I of any use?"—and make up our minds that we are not.... It is never a question of being of use, but of being of value to God Himself.

Oswald Chambers

December 2012

Somehow it goes on. Life.

And I rise from that quilted bed to the smell of burgers frying and Trent calling "Suppertime."

I rise and I sit with my boys at a table that seems to have expanded since losing the other two, and they're far across, and I stretch my hands and we hold each other, gripping, as I say grace.

Kasher in the booster seat, clapping when we finish.

It's hard to eat. I pick at the salad slowly with my fork, knowing Trent is watching with a worried expression because when life gets hard I stop eating. It's easier to be starving than to be sad; I'd rather feel the gnawing of the insides of my stomach instead of the gnawing of my heart. It's like an elastic band, one wrapped around your wrist that you snap when you start to feel angry or upset, only it's food.

And you keep doing it, you keep skipping desserts or snacks and picking at suppers, you keep being busy feeding the children and not yourself until one night when your husband pulls you close beneath the sheets. And he looks at you in the lamplight and says, "Are you eating enough, Emily?"

You think about the restless nights and you think about the two crackers you ate for lunch and you say, "No—No, I'm not. I'm sorry. I will fix that."

And you go upstairs, then, and you cut yourself a thick piece of homemade bread and slather it with peanut butter. Because you're not going back. You're not going back to those ghostlike years when you forgot how good food tasted.

"Mommy, are you sad?" Aiden is sitting by my elbow, now, at the supper table, and I shove the food into my mouth and wipe at my eyes.

Shake my head, swallow. "A little. But don't worry, honey— I'm not sad because of anything you or Kasher or Daddy did; I love you, buddy," and I keep eating, one bite at a time, because of him, and the little boy across from him too, and the man who made me supper.

"Don't let the world tell you who you are," Trent says quietly across the meal. "You will always be something big to us, Emily— you will never be more famous to us than you are right now."

A car is pulling in; lights shining on the kitchen window and Aiden leaps out of his chair. "He's here!" he cries, runs to the front door to meet Danny.

And I know that no matter what, these boys need to keep visiting us, because it's not just them we're helping. It's our own sons, and every day Aiden says he misses Danny. So we invite the world in and pull off their winter boots and feed them some

burgers and Trent's homemade fries, and we give them baths—
four to a tub, and they're all limbs and yelling and Kasher's in
it now too—he pokes his belly button and chortles and we're
family again.

The table full again, our house alive again—like we've all been
kissed by the sun.

And I almost forget—until the boys are in bed. The rejection
letter. The family that wants to sue me.

And I feel like I've been sucker punched by God.

Morning comes as it always does, like a tall woman at a clothes-
line, pinning up the skies, and I rub my eyes and walk to the com-
puter and write to my publisher. Tell him about the upset family.
I write to my agent, ask her what I should do about my novel.
The boys on the couch, lined up in their footy pajamas, watching
Backyardigans and it's toast and chocolate spread for breakfast.
The sun blinking across the snowy fields.

And somehow we keep on. We laugh and have tickle fights and
we do time-outs and stories; the boys get wrapped up in winter
gear to play in the snow for five minutes before stumbling in from
the minus degrees begging for hot chocolate, and then we lay out
the mittens and hats and scarves by the fire and it's snack time,
and Trent and I breathe and I try not to think about yesterday.

He grabs me by the window, pulls me close, and I can feel his
heartbeat beneath his shirt and he says, "I love you," even as the
boys are screaming over toys in the office and soon we'll be pulling
children off one another, but for a moment, I am held.

And even in his arms I think about my dad, and all the hours
he poured into sermons in that office chair, into visiting people
for meager pay, into finding us toys and televisions at the dump—
we loved Dump Day, like Christmas, with all of the salvageable
items people threw away—and I think about Mum, making homemade granola and bread and stitching up threadbare clothing and

shopping at Salvation Army and I wonder aloud, "Where is the blessing?"

"It is here, around us," Trent says now, into my hair. "God is blessing us, Emily, and he's blessed your dad too—look, all of his children are believers. Maybe you didn't have a lot of stuff, but blessing isn't stuff. Blessing isn't book contracts. The prosperity gospel isn't the gospel." He takes me by the shoulders, looks into my eyes. "Blessing is people. It's you, me, these children."

I take a deep breath. He traces the tattoo on my neck, the one I got last year in the shape of an S that represents the Holy Spirit—the Helper. I see the Spirit nurturing, comforting, even as the Father and the Son challenge and lead.

"You are a blessing, Emily," says Trent, "to me, to your children—don't let writing become a burden to you. Don't let it become something you have to do. I want you to want to do it, and lately you've been crying more than you've been happy."

I feel like a red tricycle in snow. Out of place and obvious, ashamed, and "I just want you to be proud of me."

I want to make money like a grown woman, I want to be more than a mother, more than a wife, but "I am proud of you," Trent says now. "I've never been prouder."

The following week a friend of mine—a counselor whom I haven't spoken with in months—emails me to ask if I'd consider writing a book with her for fathers and daughters.

She has a publisher who is interested. And I read her email and then I close my laptop and walk away because prayer isn't coming easily these days, and my hopes have been ravaged.

Eventually I open the computer and type "Yes" with a listless spirit, a soul just flapping in the wind.

So advent continues, in spite of Christmas passing. The waiting.

But still, grace.

And even as we type out a proposal and come up with a working title, my friend invites me to Portland, to her home, to work on the book in person.

She pays for half the ticket, and I book it online.

And Portland is the start of a whole new chapter.

18

Meeting Abba

Grown up, and that is a terribly hard thing to do. It is much easier to skip it and go from one childhood to another.

F. Scott Fitzgerald

January 2013

I fly from Edmonton to Portland the morning of January 11, the sky scribbled with purple and pink like children's crayons.

The flight is scheduled for 6:30 a.m., my car tucked in valet parking and me with a yellow hiking bag and an ill-fitting leather jacket, a cardigan, and a leather purse. I have a black hat on my bleached hair, and looking at pictures later, I think I appeared as defeated as I felt. Like a hobo mama, I carried it all on my back, my shoulders curved and my eyes emptied.

I am wanting. I've spent every love dollar I have on those boys, on those eleven months, and I still believed in the prosperity lie, that God would bless us materially if we obeyed him—what I yet don't know is, he wants more for me.

I spend the plane ride silent, hunched over, sleeping for a few minutes then waking to the attendant bumping my elbow. Turn on my laptop, type a few words on the book we are going to discuss, thinking, *Why try, when God doesn't return my calls?*

The ground in Portland is dusted with snow, and the temperature around zero. This is Oregon's winter—compared to our five-foot drifts and minus thirty-five degrees Celsius.

It is 9:50—the plane has touched down a little early—and Michelle will arrive at ten. I wait outside the baggage claim, in the corner, in the shadows, because I don't want to be seen. I smell like three o'clock in the morning. I smell like stale coffee and airplane peanuts. And I am not sure why I'm here.

God gave me a vision of Michelle months ago, of a woman in scarves who laughs a lot—he told me she would be my mentor. And then she wrote me in December and I recognized her from my dream, this counselor I'd met years earlier at an eating disorders conference.

She pulls up to the curb at ten o'clock sharp in her silver Jetta and her skin glows, her black hair swooped back and her blue eyes tastefully lined and sparking with life. She's wearing a long cashmere scarf, a black-and-white tweed coat, slim black pants, and black boots, and she doesn't say anything about my cardigan and leather jacket, my white running shoes and my yellow hiking bag, and we dump that bag in the trunk and take off.

"So, how are you?" Michelle looks at me and her voice is throaty and full, and when she laughs she does so with her whole body. She is vibrant and stunning and knows everyone in town, every business and trendy store—and on our way downtown we pull up beside a studio, the studio of Michelle's friend, his canvases stacked by the window, and we peek inside the windows but it is closed. She knows I am an artist, that I will appreciate the way he's structured his studio with spray-painted pipes and random antiques.

She tells me about his art, about his life, because Michelle cares. She is fifty-two and single and leads a group for men, mentoring fathers in their relationships with daughters, out of her home.

When we get back to the car, she says my shoulders are bent and that I look sad.

I say, "It's been a hard month."

Michelle nods, makes a lane change and the trees still cling to green here, even in winter. They've lost some leaves but you can still see remnants of August.

"I know, honey," she says. "We're going to talk all about that. But first I think we need some breakfast, don't you?"

So Michelle takes me to a brick restaurant with high ceilings and funky art, fair-trade coffee and free-range eggs. Indie music on the stereo, couples leaning in across rough wooden tables and I am falling hard for Portland and it isn't even noon. We eat massive plates of eggs with onions and peppers and homemade toast and drink tumblers of fresh-squeezed orange juice.

And we think about going back to Michelle's place and writing, because that is why I've come, but instead we go shopping.

She drives me downtown, this woman with the sparkling blue eyes, black hair, and scarves, who jokes about her relationship with "Jorge," her Big Gulp cup that she keeps filled with Diet Coke.

"You know Diet Coke has aspartame, which can give you cancer," I say as Michelle refills Jorge at the nearest 7-11.

She sighs. "Yes, but, I'm single. Jorge is the only man I have. So I'm willing to take the chance."

I laugh, offer to give Jorge the front seat as we walk back to the car but Michelle says he can do with a change of scenery, puts the giant cup between us.

Portland has thrift stores, and good ones, within walking distance from each other. The clothes tastefully displayed and high-end stuff too, and there is one store where I trade in my leather jacket—they take it right off my hands—and in its place I choose a long, soft, hooded beauty that ties around the waist.

I ask Michelle to help me pick out some outfits because she has such class, but she says she trusts me. And when I try on skinny jeans and dress pants and loose-fitting tops and suit jackets, she says, "Look, see, you know what looks good! You don't need me," because I've doubted myself my whole life. And she can see that I need more than an outfit.

I tell her my hunched shoulders are genetic. "Me, my dad, and my grandmother, we all slouch," but Michelle just shakes her head, takes me back to her mansion of a home that she uses for ministry.

Her house sits on a corner lot, rising tall with white siding, and inside everything is clean and trendy. Abstract paintings on the walls, soft blankets in baskets, plump pillows and long couches, an open kitchen and wide windows, hardwood and thick rugs. A piano.

The rooms smell like vanilla and Michelle tells me to take off my shoes, head on upstairs—and there is my bed, at the top of the curved staircase, a soft mattress with a mahogany frame, quilts, pillows, a gift basket on the side table filled with dark chocolate, candles, lotion, and bath salts, and she's even laid out slippers and a robe for me.

I cry.

I sit on the edge of that soft bed and I cry.

Because it's been so long.

Just a long stretch of year—of nonstop caring for five some-one elses. And here, it is my turn. Someone is taking care of me. Someone is telling me to take a bath, to light a candle. Those are my orders. And when I am ready, she says, I can come down and she'll make me some tea.

I take a bath. All foamy like the movies, the bubbles reaching my chin and I feel guilty, just lying there, but then, in the quiet of that bathroom with its white sink and white fluffy towels and blackberry candle, I hear my heavenly Father's voice and it is unmistakable.

I want to bless you, he says. *This weekend, it's for you—I want to show you how much I delight in you. Let me.*

Eventually I rise from the water, drain the tub, rub lotion into my legs and pull on some sweats. Take the stairs down into the living room with its fireplace and open windows, and Michelle makes me a mug of cinnamon apple spice tea.

And that mug of tea—in addition to the slippers waiting by my bed, and the chocolates, soaps, and lotions she's packaged as a welcome present—it opens me up like an old yellow letter just longing to be read.

We sit on her couches.

"Can I tell you what God showed me, right before I came here?" I say to Michelle, the mug warm in my hands.

She nods. "Of course, please do."

And I tell her about me having gone for a run, because that's always when God catches up with me, and how he showed me the Trinity: that we were to be reborn into the family of the Trinity, that God is our Father, Jesus our Brother, and the Holy Spirit—a Mother who nurtures and guides us, and that Christ came down to show us this, at Christmas. He didn't just come to offer a free pass to heaven, he came to bring us a family.

Michelle sits quietly, and when I am finished she says, "I've got books and papers on everything you just told me, and God showed it all to you one afternoon on a run."

I don't say anything.

And that's when she asks me about my family.

That's when she asks about the little girl Emily, and has that little girl ever been seen or heard by her own dad?

Because we are there to write a book for women who find it hard to call God *father*, a book that will help wounded daughters find their way home and I just break down, set the mug on the coffee table.

Tell Michelle all about the past month, about the rejection from the publisher, about the lawsuit with the family, about God's whisper to me in the shower, and how, in the end, he wasn't there for me. In spite of everything I'd done for him—all of those papers and speeches and art and published poetry—when really, all I'd wanted was for my daddy to pick me up and hold me close and tell me I didn't have to do any of that because I was worth more than any grade.

I ask Michelle, then, if she will pray with me.

And she does more than that. She goes to war for me.

We spend close to three hours in healing prayer together. My friend a counselor and me a thirty-two-year-old woman with a seven-year-old heart. The little girl inside of me shouting for the years I've tried to silence her.

And I never saw this coming because my dad and I are good now. We're friends now, but we didn't used to be. And that little girl, the one who'd felt ignored by her pastor-father, needed to be heard. Seen. And I needed my mentor to take me to that wounded place.

So she does, this woman who saw this hunched-over writer and knew it wasn't genetic.

Michelle says, "Where's Jesus?"

And he's there, in a garden, waiting for me, this little girl in a white dress hiding behind a tree, and I step out and he takes my hand. In that garden full of ivy and berries, the smell of hyacinth and apple blossoms, he leads me to Abba, gently pulling, because I don't want to go and yet I am tired of fighting.

And there he is—the God of the universe—running toward me even as Jesus tugs me up heaven's path, Abba's beard and cloak flying in the wind—and he takes me in his arms.

I cry and I rest, bang my tiny fists against his chest and then I rest again. And I pull away and see the kindest eyes, the most loving smile, and then lean in, rest some more.

And when I am ready, God shows me a room he's prepared for me in heaven, and in it is the largest piece of canvas I've ever seen and all the paints money can buy and he tells me I can paint if I want to. But I don't have to. And with this, I pick up a brush and I begin to spread the color across the canvas and Abba, he just watches me and smiles and applauds and soon I drop the brush and run back to him because there is no greater pleasure than being in his arms.

I don't need to do anything. I don't need to prove anything, anymore. I don't need to hear that I am beautiful or smart or powerful, because Abba's very presence says I am perfect, accepted, loved, redeemed, cherished, delighted in, and sung over. God wants to spend time with me. That is enough.

And in my mind's eye I see Jesus, the Son, preparing tools for me to take on a journey. He is handing the tools to the Holy Spirit, because she is going with me. And there they are, my family: my Father, my Brother, and my Mother.

And the Father, just holding me. "When you're ready," Abba whispers. "You can stay here as long as you want. Don't leave until you're ready." And for the first time in my life, I rest. For the first time in my life, I don't need to perform; I don't need to prove anything. I don't need to worry about someone losing interest in me or getting frustrated with me.

And when I finally stand up from that prayer, three hours later, the shadows outside lengthening and the tea grown cold, Michelle takes me to the mirror in her downstairs bathroom and shows me my reflection. "What do you see?" she says.

My face is glowing. "I look younger," I say.

She smiles. "I think you look wiser." And then she points to my shoulders. "And you're standing tall. Confident. You're no longer ashamed."

I look again.

I see a girl who is no longer running.

I see a girl who has come home.

To a Father who never stopped loving her.

The next day I meet with my agent, Shauna.

She meets me at Michelle's door, because they both live in Portland, and she compliments my new jacket, my scarf, and then she leans on my shoulder as though she's weary. I know I must seem taller, because she's never leaned on me before.

And then I climb into her vehicle, and we're going for yogurt—the kind you pour out of the wall, through a faucet, swirled high like ice cream and then you pile on toppings, fruit and chocolate—and you sit in the corner lit with sun and talk about things like dreams, and writing, and the future.

But before we get there Shauna turns to me, with her short blonde hair and her wise eyes—this agent who used to be in the marines—and she says, "I have good news for you."

I grip the edge of the car seat because it's been so long. "Good news?" My knuckles are white because I'm already waiting for the letdown. "What is it?"

Shauna smiles, turns a corner, and I'm waiting. "There's an editor with Baker Books who contacted me over the holidays. He reads your blog, and he asked if you'd be willing to write a travel memoir for him."

I stumble over the words *travel memoir*; I'm not sure what that means, but first I need to know—and all I can think of is the past month, crying on the bed, holding myself, doubting that I've ever been able to hear from God—the same God who told me he was preparing an editor for me.

"What's his name?" I say, my breath coming short.

She pauses. "His name is John."

19

Talitha Koum

Look for God. Look for God like a man with his head on fire looks for water.

Elizabeth Gilbert

April 2013

It's been thirty-six days and my cycle is thirty-four. We've been trying for three months and I'm in the bathroom at 11:03 p.m. near the end of April, one week before leaving for Nebraska to speak at a retreat on how creating has saved me.

The bathroom window is a black rectangle of sky, a soft glow from the night-light, the crackle of a fire because we still light one at night, and Trent already asleep in bed—the boys in theirs, and I love the quiet. I sink hard into it, like a featherbed, and it's in this quiet that I hear my Abba's voice. *Stop drinking*, he says. I'd had a glass of wine that night.

You are pregnant, he says, *and she will have a prophetic spirit, and be musical, just like you.*

I haven't taken a pregnancy test yet, but I clap quietly in the dark, flush the toilet, slip back into bed, and dream of the little girl we'd had visions of a year earlier. The one with chubby cheeks and big brown eyes, singing down the hallway.

And in the morning I take the test—it turns bright pink right away, like a sunrise, and Trent's on the phone with his dad when I show it to him and shout, "We're pregnant! God said we are and look! It's true!"

So it begins, me telling the world our unashamed news, and we start to receive baby gifts in the mail nine months early, because God said it was so. He spoke life over my womb, and there it is, and she is coming. Our daughter.

I leave for Nebraska a week later and the nausea hits in the mornings, but every time I smile, knowing it is her—a cacophony of female cells forming into prophecy and music. I pack my plastic bag of prenatal pills and folic acid and I've cut down on coffee and am already protectively placing a hand on my stomach when I speak about her.

I arrive in Ashland, Nebraska, to a dry heat and Arin—the founder of the retreat—picks me up at the airport. She's short with curly hair and a laugh that falls graciously, a kind of rain that soaks everything around it, and we talk about God on the way to the Carol Joy Holling Retreat, surrounded by wide open spaces—a starlit sky and the arms of branches holding leaves and blossoms. I fall into bed that night, and come morning I set up my art in the room where I'll be speaking, find my way to the coffee room for some breakfast, and it's there I meet up with my friend Heather. And she goes on a walk with me, and we end up talking about her dream to have children and how it never happened.

"I realized one day that maybe God wanted me to have different kinds of daughters—ones that I raise through my writing," she says, soft eyes searching mine as we walk the path by the pond—there are people fishing, some on the dock, and paths crisscross the hills rolling up to the sky. Like a rainbow of scruffy grass and yellow flowers, rising.

I tell her about doctors saying I wouldn't have children either, and the pastor praying. "I don't deserve any," I say, tearing. "I wrecked my body and here he's given me another one—and I just don't know why."

Heather smiles as I talk. We're reaching the entrance and bloggers are arriving. "He knows what we need," she says quietly. "He has a plan for all of us. I love how our stories are all so different, yet they all speak of him and what he is doing."

We enter a busy place then, full of handshakes and hugs and the smell of perfume. I speak later that weekend on art, drinking mugs of tea because my voice is going hoarse, and all along, even as I look to the notes in my hands—the ones scribbled about my anorexia and the way I painted and wrote poems to find God—then out, to the faces of women peering up at me, I feel as though a cavalry is riding through my chest, charging. I feel a rising, like the hills beyond the window, a need to help these women know who they are as Abba's daughters, because I remember her.

The seven-year-old me sitting at her wooden desk, writing those words as straight and neat as possible and scratching the side of her head, blue ink staining her temple, wondering how perfect it had to be to make the pain go away. The pain of feeling unseen and unheard.

Afterward, these women talk to me—tell me their dreams.

"When I was a little girl, I dreamed that I could touch God," one says in a faraway voice. "I would swing. I would swing so high and try to touch the sky, because I thought if I touched the sky, I could maybe touch God."

She leans in, her brown hair wavy and her eyes bright. "And I would sing. I would sing long and loud, hoping that maybe, if I sang enough, he might hear me."

I swallow.

When do we stop trying to touch God? Trying to get him to hear us? Believing that if we wanted, we could do the impossible?

And I remember how, earlier that weekend, I had been standing in worship, my hands outstretched as Jaime, the man in the cap with the earrings, strummed his guitar and we sang "Holy, Holy, Holy." And I closed my eyes as I stretched my hands to the ceiling and I've never reached so high.

And suddenly, with my eyes closed, I saw him.

My Abba Father, reaching down from heaven, trying to grasp my hand.

His face, so eager.

And for a brief moment, the chasm between humanity and the divine didn't seem so wide.

A few hours later I am signing books in the foyer of the retreat center. My newest book, *Mom in the Mirror*, fresh off the press in hard cover, and *Chasing Silhouettes*, the eating disorder guide I've had to reprint, and I'm bowed low over the pages, signing, when a hand taps me on my shoulder.

It's a lady from one of my workshops, and she slips a folded piece of paper into my hands. "I felt the Lord telling me to give this message to you," she says. "I hope you don't mind."

Then she's gone among the pairs of legs and dangling purses.

When I'm done signing, I unfold the paper. "Mark 5:41," it reads. "He took her by the hand and said to her, '*Talitha koum!*' (which means 'Little girl, I say to you, get up!')."

I see her again. That little seven-year-old girl, the one with the mushroom cut, bent over her desk. And Jesus, standing beside her, holding out his hand to her—pierced and calloused.

Saying, *Talitha koum.*

Little girl, arise.

20

Fight with the Devil

The only thing necessary for the triumph of evil is for good men to do nothing.

Edmund Burke

May 2013

I am at an eating disorders conference in Nashville, Tennessee. A worship band is playing up front and we are under a pavilion. It's rained all day but is clear and quiet now, and the air feels like a soft black blanket filled with stars.

I am slotted to speak tomorrow and my talk has been planned for months, the one in which I share my story of not eating from the ages of nine to thirteen. It is all typed out and memorized so I won't make a mistake.

The band begins to play another worship song and the words and the notes pull my hands high and I am closing my eyes, wanting to somehow touch Abba like last month, in Nebraska.

"I need you," I say to God, and then, in the middle of that holy moment, I hear it. A voice that is not my Father's. A voice from the past, from four years of starving, a voice that found Jesus in the desert.

You're an affirmation junkie, it says.

My arms fall; my face does too and everything in me collapses. I had been told years earlier, by an editor, that I was an affirmation junkie. I'd thought I had let it go. I had worked long and hard to replace the lies with the truth: that I was redeemed and loved, that I was enough, that God doesn't make mistakes, and that I am a new creation, beautifully and wonderfully made.

I don't know if it's because I am tired or because I am about to get vulnerable the next day and share how God saved me from anorexia, but Satan interrupts my worship that night.

I try to walk as casually as I can away from the band and the pavilion and into the dark so no one can see my tears for the shadows.

And then I reach the creek trickling past the pavilion, and I hide in the bushes and sob, just aching and raw for how that moment was stolen from me.

I feel cheated. I'd thought those worshipful moments were somehow protected, those holy unions in which everything you've spent your life professing—all of the faith you have for God—is, for a few minutes, tangible and close.

And it is so easy to believe the lies again.

So very easy. I sob for remembering how little and insignificant I felt those years—and then, an editor's cold email after I'd asked him if he'd liked a story I'd submitted. "Has anyone ever told you that you're an affirmation junkie?" he wrote.

Sticks and stones may break my bones—but words, they kill the soul.

I sob and then pace, and the more I walk the emptier I feel. I keep begging God to step in and help, but my spirits are as low as they've ever been.

And all of a sudden, I get angry at the devil.

I yell at the night, "You robbed me of that beautiful moment! How dare you!"

My insides are throbbing with courage and the enemy has nothing on me anymore. Because I'm not afraid of him. *I know he is the father of lies and I am calling him on it.*

And in that moment I know that he who is in me is greater than he who is in the world.

I wipe my eyes and go back to the pavilion and rewrite my entire talk for the next day on a napkin because I am no longer afraid of messing it up. I am no longer scared of not having it perfect. It won't be memorized and I'll probably have to read a bunch of it. But that is okay. I just want it to be real and true and messy and raw.

I am shaking.

God's power all poured from me onto that napkin. And it is holier than any amount of raising my arms to heaven.

And when I stand on the platform the next day and give my message, the napkin all wrinkled in my hands, I feel so strong—like nothing can get me now—because I fought with the devil.

And I won.

That night, after speaking of my journey all scribbled there on my napkin, I go to the bathroom.

And there is blood, bright red, on the toilet paper.

PART 5

Daughter

What I wanted most for my daughter was that she be able to soar confidently in her own sky, whatever that may be.

Helen Claes

21

Losing Madeleine

Where you used to be, there is a hole in the world, which
I find myself constantly walking around in the daytime, and
falling in at night.

Edna St. Vincent Millay

June 2013

I used to think my babies were safest within my womb.

I've loved her since the moment God told me to stop drinking because I had life in me, he said, and I hadn't even taken the pregnancy test yet.

I got sick right away, which is good, because morning sickness lets me know my hormones are high and when I miscarried, years earlier, I hadn't felt sick at all, so this time I had nothing to worry about but still I did.

Because every mother does, and yet the Lord whispered, *Life. I've spoken life into you. And it is good*, so I believed.

And we got the baby updates. The ones telling us our child was starting to look not so fish-like.

Then, blood on the toilet paper in Tennessee.

And a couple of weeks later, I woke up on Saturday, June 8, and I lifted my two little boys from their beds and they ran off to play while I went to the washroom and found more blood in the toilet. Darker, now, than the blood in Nashville.

And dark means good, means old implantation blood, so I'm not too worried and God has spoken life over me, but still, maybe it would be wise to go into the hospital and confirm. I am secretly hoping for an ultrasound to catch a glimpse of my Madeleine.

I get that glimpse of my Madeleine as I am lying there in the emergency room, and the doctor is squinting at the screen and saying, "The baby is smaller than it should be."

But they'd said that about my second son too, and he'd turned out fine even though I bled with him, and God had spoken life over this child so I just sort of smiled to myself and let the doctor worry.

They took some blood tests and sent me home. I was sure everything would be okay. But the bleeding didn't stop. And Sunday I could barely walk for the cramps. Trent kept reminding me of what God said, but I needed more. Because the blood was bright and I was getting scared.

So I sat on the couch and I waited for my miracle.

I begged God for an answer. I said, "Lord, please tell me, what is going to happen to this baby?"

And I heard, *As surely as the sun is shining, I love you—and your baby will live.*

The sun didn't stop shining once that day, even as storm clouds rolled in and out again. I kept checking the sky and the sun still shining and then at five o'clock my family doctor called and said my hormone levels were really high and dated the baby at even more developed than we'd thought.

He said the other doctor's measurements had just been off, and the baby looked fine, and Trent said, "See?" and I did.

I saw, even though the cramping increased and the clotting began and I had to go to the hospital.

And the doctor did a spec and said my cervix was still closed, and I nodded because I knew everything was going to be fine. I knew it, even at midnight when the clots got bigger and my whole abdomen, convulsing. I called Trent from the hospital bed and he prayed with me, and we told the Lord we trusted his promise that our baby would live.

And then at 1:30 a.m. I went to the toilet again and it felt like all of my insides slid into the bowl and the nurse was very quiet as she looked at my clots, even after I'd returned to the bed. And then she came out and said, "It looks like we've found some tissue."

I stared at her blankly because God was going to save my baby.

"Is everything okay?" I said, and she shook her head and then walked over to me and in her hand was the sac.

Perfect and round and "Is my baby in there?" I said.

She nodded.

"The product of your conception is in this sac," she said.

I sat on the bed. I didn't know how the Lord was going to save Madeleine now but for a minute I thought he still could. Because the sac was so perfect and the hormones were high and I'd had morning sickness.

"Your baby measured where it should have, but your body thought it was a foreign object and rejected it," the doctor said. He'd come into the room and was standing with his hands in his pockets. "I'm so sorry."

The nurse brought me chamomile tea and warm blankets.

I called Trent and he was half asleep. I told him and he said, "Oh Emily. I'm so sorry. It's going to be okay." And then the nurse left the room, and I sat up straight and started to cry because suddenly the room was so very empty. Not even God was with me anymore.

I'd always been able to talk to God.

But he'd tricked me. He'd said my baby would live and now it was in a test tube being shipped off to a lab to be examined and I couldn't stop bleeding.

I hadn't just lost a child. I'd lost my Father. It felt as though the whole universe had been sucked dry of spiritual force and everything was just kind of left hanging, lifeless, like a sheet in the dull heat of summer.

The next morning the doctor said I could go home and the rest of the tissue slipped silently into the toilet at my mother-in-law's house.

I sat on the couch and held my boys who squirmed because I was gripping too tight.

Death makes you do that.

Grip life like it's the handle of a chair.

Marge made me eggs over-easy, on toast, and I turned on my laptop while I ate. For the first time in a long time I didn't say grace. There was nothing gracious about this moment, and my arm rose and fell, bringing food to my mouth like some robotic extension.

I didn't know how to pray because I couldn't trust the One I was praying to, and I opened my email. A friend had written.

Dearest Em, the Lord put you on my heart early this morning. Holding you there. Just holding you. And I want to whisper this one word I believe he spoke, and I hope it comforts you as it comforted me. It's simply this: every word he spoke to you about this baby stands. *I know it doesn't make sense. That it even sounds crazy. But I honestly believe that, in God's upside-down kingdom, a lot of things pan out very differently from our expectations. I won't say more than that, but only want you to know that you didn't mishear him. And, because he is all grace, I believe the day will come when you see with your own eyes the fulfillment of all the Lord has spoken. All.*

I told her I felt tricked. Betrayed. And she wrote back immediately:

Not tricked or betrayed, but rather loved and trusted by him to endure as seeing what is unseen. He will not let you fall.

My face fell into my hands. Marge reading to the boys on the couch, and me hiding behind the screen and crying into my palms. *He will not let you fall.*

All I could see was the sac. So perfect and round and whole. But my faith—it was there too. Perfect and round and whole. And miscarried.

"Put me back together, Abba," I prayed. Closed the laptop. Wiped my cheeks and rose to take the boys home.

My womb aching like an amputated limb.

My friends drive from the city, bring me guacamole and fajitas. They bring dark chocolate and they cook lunch for me, and then they give me a tree.

A tree for Madeleine.

And one of my friends, Sarah, takes my hands and she looks in my eyes. "I know it can't replace her, but it will grow, and remind you of her—that she is still alive, with God, and in your heart."

Madeleine's tree.

They pull away, back to the city, and I take the sapling, buckets of rainwater, and the boys, and we walk to the backyard. We kneel a few feet from the apple tree where we've buried our guinea pig Mr. Nibbles, who died of heatstroke and age, and our duckling, the one the nanny brought to us, and we plant Madeleine's tree. The boys' fingernails filling with soil and they quietly pat the ground, making a soft bed for their sister to lie in.

I pour the rainwater, and then we sit. As though waiting for some kind of manifestation of growth, some kind of thank-you from the tree.

Then I take the boys' soiled hands and we pray around that sapling. We pray God will take good care of Madeleine in heaven and us here on earth, and thank you, Jesus, for friends who bring us guacamole.

Amen.

22

A Letter to My Unborn Daughter

It's so much darker when a light goes out than it would have been if it had never shone.

John Steinbeck

Dear Madeleine,

I dreamt of you one year before you came to us.

Your daddy and I, we dreamt of you one spring day when the daffodils were bursting yellow in the garden. Are there gardens there in heaven? No doubt, full of the finest flowers, all bright like the acrylic colors I use on canvas, and they'll never die there, where you are.

But I am here, in the Dutch village where we live, where you grew for eight weeks in my womb. We saw you before you arrived, chubby-cheeked and brown-haired with your daddy's hazel eyes and he didn't tell me. Your daddy didn't say he'd seen you with his mind's eye as he biked through Neerlandia, because he was waiting to see if you'd visit me too.

And you did.

I run every day down a rambling road by our place, and you would like our house I think, all large and sprawling and filled with boys. There's a lot of space here, a lot of green, and deer sometimes wander across our yard. One morning we found a moose asleep on our front lawn. Coyotes howl at night. It's quiet here mostly, a good kind of place to hear birds and God.

I saw you in my mind, that day on that road under a sky that was stretched taut like my belly when I held your brothers. And you were so beautiful, my little girl, and you were singing. You were two, and you wore a white dress and you were walking down the hall toward the kitchen where I bake bread every week and feed your brothers lunch and you have two of them, you know. Two brothers who look like each other and Aiden's always putting his arms around Kasher and saying, "Kasher's my best friend," and they would have been good to you.

And you have another sister, who's in heaven. She was our first, and her nickname was "Agi," which is Korean for "baby." I trust she'll find you, and take care of you until I come, my sweetheart.

You were singing as you came down the hall, the wall filled with photos and paintings and at one point I'd thought perhaps you and I would paint together. At the kitchen table just to make your daddy mad because I always leave streaks of paint on the wood and he doesn't get really mad, honey, he's the best man I know. He's a math and Bible teacher and he's the kind of father who plays with his children. And he treated you like a princess when you were with us. Always kissing my belly and talking to you about how he'd never let you date.

But he would have. Eventually. Maybe when you turned thirty, but you only turned two months with us and then my body failed you, daughter. You were healthy and strong and somehow I let you go. I thought I was holding on and then the nurses showed me your sac in their hands, and I shook my head fiercely because you were still inside of me. You still are.

And yet I know you're with your heavenly Father now too, and that makes me glad, in a way that throws me into tears every week.

And you were singing in that white dress, walking down the hall and your brothers wrestling in the living room and then you came around the corner. They saw you and ran up to you and picked you up and you laughed. Your laugh sounded like a thousand birds taking flight, a rush of wings.

I still hear it, Madeleine. I still hear your laugh and we planted a tree for you, a few days after I left the hospital. It grows in our backyard, a tiny lodgepole pine. One week after we lost you, the boys and I ate ice cream with you out in the backyard by that baby tree. We sat by the tree and talked about you, because they'd known God was giving them a sister. And we laughed with you there by that pine, licking vanilla as it ran down our fingers and we said goodbye in the same way I say hello to you every morning because you're my daughter, Madeleine. You're in heaven, yes, but you'll always be with me here on earth too.

So I thought I would write to you. Tell you a bit about me, and about your brothers and about your dad. About the God who made you, who sees you every day now, and about what it means to be a woman.

Because you are one, Madeleine, inasmuch as you are spirit you are female and I think we've lost a bit of what it means to be that. The beauty of what it means to bear the curves of the world.

I think we've lost what it means to take pride in womanhood. In being us. In having soft hearts and hands and arms that open. Down here we're all Eve. We're all taking from the tree, struggling to believe God loves us, that he wants good things for us.

So often, though, those good things feel a lot like pain.

And I'm hurting because I can't be with you, but I'm so glad you're there. You won't have to go through an eating disorder because you feel confused or alone. You won't have to cut or cry. You can rest now. You can know who you are now. And who you are is loved.

And you can call me Mommy if you like, and I will call you Maddy, and this is how it begins, darling. Because my body may have lost you, but you found a way to my heart, dear girl. And there you grow.

I read somewhere that heaven has a nursery. A pastor who sees visions saw a nursery in heaven, with angels watching over thousands of aborted and miscarried babies. And when mothers go to heaven, they have the chance to raise their lost child again.

You and me, again, my girl.

This keeps me holding on to the shaky ladder that extends from here to God.

So go to sleep, my daughter. Feel my kisses on your forehead, let the angels sing you lullabies, and soon, my daughter, you will see me.

And I will never let you go.

Always and forever,

Mommy

23

Going Home

And you, my father, there on the sad height,
Curse, bless me now with your fierce tears, I pray.
Do not go gentle into that good night.
Rage, rage against the dying of the light.

Dylan Thomas

August 2013

Dishes splayed like tired white hands by the sink in the condo. Dad had rented it for us in Collingwood, two hours from Toronto in the southern heat of Ontario.

My sister Allison's wedding was last week, a lace and sunflower affair under the laughing leaves of the maples in Mum and Dad's backyard.

We'd flown east mid-July, and I'd stood in my crimson brides-maid's dress holding a sunflower, Allison's steel-headed piano teacher at the keyboard and Allison and her German fiancé with the quiet laugh and the gentle hands underneath the trellis. Dad, behind them, marrying them, as he did for us ten years earlier. Wearing the same black suit, and Mum in a navy number, her cheeks rosy in the crowd.

Uncle Rupert—one of Dad's older brothers—stood in the back among the trees like the thinnest of branches, his shirt and pants hanging because he would die a month later from leukemia. But he came, and he stood shaky and he cried, Aunt Millie beside him. Holding him, her arms strong from chopping wood and running the farm.

And after the wedding Mum, Dad, and the kids drove to Collingwood for a week—Allison and Philipp on their honeymoon and the rest of us on our annual vacation.

We've been here at the timeshare seven days now, and I'm pulling cereal boxes and loaves of bread and half-eaten packages of cookies from the cupboard in the condo, Keith and Darcie's kids jumping with mine on the sofas and the laundry still a heap by the dryer.

"Where is Dad?" I mumble under my breath. He said we'd be leaving at ten and that he'd try and come early to help us pack up.

Dad had stayed with Mum in a condo a few blocks down, and we met every day for breakfast around the long table here, and it was a week full of tennis and long runs down rambling paths in the woods, splashing in a pool and watching Mum slip on a new swimsuit and join us—the first time I remembered her wearing a swimsuit.

"You've seen her in a swimsuit before—you must have, on our trip to Arizona?" Keith said, my younger brother who's taller than me, his bearded face scrunched in memory.

I hadn't. I just remembered seeing turtlenecks and long skirts and sweaters, the way Mum's skin was always hidden. But I was sick back then, when I was eleven, the butt of my swimsuit empty and flapping as I walked into the water, my ribs scaled like a cleaned fish. I didn't remember much of anything except hunger pangs.

I'm folding clothes and Kasher's crying, Aiden's not wanting to leave, and Keith's kids are hungry, so I find some Cheerios, set them out on the table for them to eat, and Dad's still not here and it's ten minutes to. The fridge needs to be emptied, the dishes washed and put away, the clothes packed, and I'm fighting back tears as I fold.

Darcie comes in and takes her kids and we both glance at the clock. She makes a remark, "I thought Dad would be here to help us," and I nod at this pixie-haired, petite girl with three kids in tow.

"I know," I say. "Me too."

And even as I'm packing and sweeping and cleaning the condo we've all shared for a week, I'm thinking of the little girl, the one who was always waiting for Dad at church, to finish shaking the last hand, to finish counting the offering and cleaning up the pews, to finish—so that we could go home.

"Can we go now?" I'd say, watching all the families drive off to eat at restaurants on Sunday, knowing we had a forty-five-minute drive home.

"Not yet, Emily—almost." He wouldn't look at me as he said it, his laughter lines gone, all spent on vacation. He had time to laugh on vacation. He had time to camp and to roast marshmallows and to read us stories by the fire, but the rest of the year church came first.

I picture him now, writing his sermon or studying something online in his condo, and *Where are you when I need you?* The suitcases full and the boxes packed with groceries and Trent and Keith taking load after load downstairs to the cars while I wipe counters and turn off lights.

Grab the last box full of groceries and the bottle of ketchup falls in the hall, and then a bag of bread and Kasher and Aiden crying because they want Mommy to pick them up down the long flights of stairs.

Me, sitting on my bed in my room, a skinny twelve-year-old staring at her pastel walls and the posters of Michael W. Smith and DC Talk, my fingers wrapping around my wrists, wondering, *Where are you, Dad? Why won't you ask what's wrong?*

I don't remember him once coming into my bedroom.

We make it to the bottom of the stairs, out the doors, see Dad's car there, Mum in the passenger seat with her pink hat pulled down to her ears, and the air smells of hot asphalt. Keith and Trent there, laughing, Darcie strapping their kids into their blue four-door and Dad steps out of the car.

"Where were you?" I cry.

The box drops. Everyone stops and turns.

My hair in my eyes, blurred with tears, and I know there are children watching but there's a child inside me too and she's upset. "We needed you this morning, Dad—why couldn't you come? We had to clean up all by ourselves and pack everything with five kids and half the stuff was groceries we all used this week, and where were you?"

Dad's scratching the back of his head, saying, "I was late, I didn't know," and everyone's silent, and then Trent says, "Emily, do you really want to do this?"

I turn to them. To the people watching, say, "Oh great, now you can say, 'Emily did it again. Emily lost it on family vacation. She's such a mess.' I bet you're happy."

I turn and run, trying to be faster than their stares, into the building, toward the bathroom and a woman is standing there, sees my swollen face and I turn, duck into a corner and crouch down and sob into my lap.

Wishing I could somehow become as two-dimensional as the wall behind me, and people coming and going and not saying anything.

I am the same girl who would scream and then run to her room and slam the door and wonder why no one followed her. Why they cared enough to read her journal but not enough to sit and ask her what was the matter. Why she was so hurting she couldn't eat. Why she'd rather die than pick up a fork.

Seven years ago we were at a cottage in Val-de-Bois, Quebec, the loons on the lake with canoes and children, cabins circling the quiet waters.

It was late and we were playing Power Grid, a board game I hadn't played before. I was pregnant and tired and asking Trent for advice each turn—which meant I was also winning—which ruffled Keith's feathers since he and Trent are very competitive when it comes to board games.

I was getting warm and flustered with the bickering so I opened a window—and then Dad kept using my name, over and over again.

"Emily, you shouldn't open the window."

"Dad, I just need a bit of air."

"But Emily, the bugs will come in. Emily, the light attracts the bugs. Emily (patronizing tone) Emily . . . bugs/light/don't do it, Emily."

"DAD, STOP USING MY NAME LIKE I'M FIVE YEARS OLD!"

Dad was quiet.

The boys continued to bicker and then I began to cry because I just wanted to have a nice board game where it didn't matter who won or lost.

I left the game and ran to the lake with my pregnant belly because these family gatherings, they're like reruns of an old show that you didn't quite understand the first time. And the more you watch it the more it reminds you of how much you didn't get it.

Just once, I'd like a new episode.

I wipe my face and stand, shaky, not wanting to go out there, to my boys who saw Mommy blow up at Grandpa, or the cousins, or Keith or Trent. But I do, and they're all in their cars except for Mum who comes up to me, puts her pink hat close to my forehead, puts her arms around my waist, says, "Em, I'm so sorry—it was my fault. I made Dad late this morning. Don't blame him honey—it's all me. I didn't want to leave because I was playing a game of Solitaire."

I hiccup and laugh and hug her, because it's hard to be mad at Mum's large blue eyes and flushed cheeks. And then I walk over to Dad. "I'm sorry, Emily," he says, pushing up his glasses. "I didn't realize how important it was to you that I be here."

I shake my head. "It's okay, Dad. Mum said she made you late. Please forgive me. I'm having a bad day."

We hug, and I'm learning that we all need kindness, because we're all fighting our own battles.

I smell Dad's Ivory soap skin and it reminds me of him singing me lullabies under the Congo skies, praying with me at bedtime, teaching me French and piano and recorder, driving us to the coast in a minivan without air-conditioning, setting up the tent trailer every night for us, buying us day-old donuts and fixing everything when it broke. I could always trust him to fix things.

I smell my Dad, and he smells like home.

We're back in Alberta now, pulling out of the Edmonton airport parking lot, Trent in the driver's seat and me in the backseat with the kids, holding Aiden's hand because he's shaky and tired from the five-hour flight.

And I glance at the back of Trent's head, the road before us, and I feel safe, my husband at the wheel.

Dad always brought us home.

Me, the girl tucked beside Keith, stacks of coloring books and Anne of Green Gables and Laura Ingalls Wilder and the Hardy Boys between us, stacks of years between us—the stolen kind, the kind the eating disorder had taken from us, but we also had the good years.

The ones where my brother and I would dress up in our Tickle Trunk costumes in the old Staffa house with the wide-open branches of maple trees out back, the rope swing, and later on

Dad made us girls a wooden playhouse, because he was good at doing things like that.

And on vacations, Dad would tell puns and we'd feign groans—secretly delighted he was having fun with us—driving the highway to the Maritimes, to the frothy eastern sea with its lighthouses and fish and chip shops, and all the way out west to California, in the steamed-up heat of a Chrysler minivan. Four kids in the back and *Adventures in Odyssey* on the stereo, Mum up front reading or crocheting and Dad with a faded map, its folds worn and the faint smell of sweat caused by the August sun.

I never worried, there in the backseat, because Dad would take care of us—I knew that—in the same way that he stood sentry outside my bedroom door when I couldn't sleep for the nightmares or the thunder and lightning, in the same way that he fixed everything we had with duct tape and wire.

And we'd arrive home from holidays, pulling in late to the gravel driveway, our bulging, ripped duffel bags smelling of sand and sea. I'd always pretend to be asleep, my head against Mum's hand-sewn gingham curtains. The rest of the kids piled out but I wanted Dad to lift me up and carry me into the house because I felt safest in his arms.

I would never have told him that, though, and even as I stretched taller into sixty pounds at five foot six, the skinny flesh pulled taut across muscle and bone and I yelled at him, I punched him, I hated him I said, and Dad just stood there wearily, rubbing a hand beneath his glasses, across his tired, kind eyes. He could fix everything except his own daughter. No amount of wire or duct tape, no amount of long trips with the puns and the laughter, could make up for the rest of the year when we moved from house to house, when he worked late and stayed up on the computer and gave me a peck on the cheek in the mornings when all I wanted was for him to pick me up and hold me, again.

"Emily, I wish you would listen to your mother," Dad said when Mum told him tearfully how I'd refused to eat, to follow her food charts, to drink the cod liver oil, and those were the lonely years.

Slamming my door and sitting on the edge of my immaculate bed with Cuddles my teddy bear, weighing myself and scheduling my outfits for each day of the week.

The counselor came and tried to fix things for us but that only made me angrier because I didn't want to be just a problem to be fixed or a member of the family to be controlled, to be home-schooled and told to listen and speak respectfully and to never, ever let someone see that I might be breaking.

And then God let me break, nearly die, and on that hospital bed I felt the edges of the cloth that is love, and I pulled it close. This God I'd memorized verses about, this God I'd done confirmation class for, been baptized for, this God I didn't know.

I pulled that tattered cloth close, that love, and it began to weave its way around me, cocooning me, even as my heavenly Father said he'd saved me for a purpose that was more than an empty plate. More than the digits on a scale, and I picked up that fork again and began to eat.

Even as God picked me up from the backseat of my life and carried me into healing.

When I moved back home from the hospital, Dad began to take me on dates to Ann's Café, the lamp low across his face leaning toward mine, seeing me for the first time. He began to help me with my science fair projects and math homework at the kitchen table, and my pastor-father became human.

It's all any of us ever wants. To know we're not alone.

Abba is bringing me home the same way Dad carried us in from the backseat of that rusting Chrysler, the way Trent drives us now in our red Dodge, down Yellowhead Trail toward Neerlandia.

My heavenly Father at the wheel of my life, and me—safe, there in the dark.

24

Danny and Sam

I have always found that mercy bears richer fruits than strict justice.

Abraham Lincoln

December 2013

Danny and Sam are visiting. They come every three weeks for a respite, but they're always excited to go home. Home is good now.

It's bedtime, Aiden and Kasher in the bunks, Sam in the crib—we sang "Jesus Loves Me" to him minutes ago, Aiden, Kasher, and Danny singing too, Sam's heart-shaped face beaming beneath the duvet. And I imagine that's how the angels sing over us every day, if we would only have ears.

And I've tucked Danny beneath the quilt in his bed in the guest room, which also serves as our office, with his three teddy bears. He asks me to sing the same song I sang to Sam because our greatest longing is to be someone's son or daughter. I sing "Skinnamarinky

Dinky Dink," turn out the lights, and he begs me to leave the door open, and "Where will you be, Emily?" he asks. "Will you be upstairs?"

I nod. "Yes, I'll be working in the living room right next door, Danny. Don't worry. Night night, honey."

He sighs and lies down on his pillow, the blue light from the printer blinking across the walls.

A cookie and some tea now, and Kasher's crying for the green glass of water, the one that sits beside the sink downstairs, so I go downstairs and get him some water, and then he wants me to lie with him.

"It's time for bed," I say in my firm voice.

Praying, *God, please let them sleep so I can write.*

But I'm learning. There should always be time for snuggles, so I turn back. Lie down beside Kasher, kiss the soft roundness of his cheek, and then Aiden, for a couple more minutes. He tells me stories about his flashlight, slips his small hand into mine.

Finally I climb the stairs, Trent asleep in the recliner by the fire, and from the guest room, "Emily—you there?"

Danny's voice, plaintive, like a minor chord.

"I'm here, honey, go to sleep."

He does this periodically, calling out, as though we're playing a game of Marco Polo, like sailboats in the seas of night.

I try to write, but it hurts.

This longing to conceive.

And sometimes I just have to cry, a mother's tears for all her lost children, and the whispers of the ones calling "Marco?" and you can't find them. For all the boats and the lighthouses, you can't find your babies.

It's been seven months since the miscarriage and I know some couples try for years, but it feels like that, because of the dream of her. That little girl singing down the halls of our hearts.

Danny has adult teeth now, and some gaps where his gums smile wide, and he prays to the Father, Son, and Holy Ghost because he goes to a Catholic school.

"Emily?" he calls again, after a while.

"Still here," I reply, and I smile, the lamp on the bookshelf glowing like an altar call. Some prayers have been answered with an exclamation mark; it's been a year, and Danny and Sam are stretching tall because they're finally growing roots.

I touch my womb, and it's not empty. It's full of promise.

"Abba?" I whisper.

Still here, he replies.

It awakens, the dawn, with a slow blinking eye, and finds me packing for Africa.

I leave in a week, for nine days—four days in flight, five days on the ground, part of a motley crew of bloggers with World Help. We've been asked to tell the stories of orphans, rescued from the slums of Katwe, Uganda, of children in the north, in Gulu—forced into the Lord's Resistance Army when they were just five years old, some as soldiers and others as child-mothers, now learning skills like welding and sewing, the gospel woven into their lives like a new garment, but oh.

I cry as I pack for all the horror. Being pulled from your hut in the dark, forced to shoot your brother so you'll be shamed into not returning home, and I can't bring myself to watch *Hotel Rwanda*. We'll be going there next, flying to Kigali, traveling by bus to talk with the widows of the genocide. Women who've seen their sons and daughters and husbands killed, who've been banished from their country and then slowly welcomed back, and the government created this village for them, where they take care of orphans. The babies strapped to the backs of grandmothers with long pieces of cloth.

I don't know then—even as I fold my jeans—how the genocide museum will undo me.

How I'll run from the museum, past the concrete gravesites, up to the rose bushes whose flowers are strangely bright. Taking vain hope in a blossom that has fallen but remains brilliantly crimson.

How I'll sit down on a cement step and cry.

A Rwandan priest who's also been at the museum passing me, shaking his head, whispering "*Apolli, apolli.*" It sounds like, "Appalling, appalling."

And me thinking, *There is so much room for error in the human spirit.*

I'll sit there and sob, wondering what the answer is. And knowing somehow if there's that much room for evil in the human spirit—there's also that much room for goodness.

Later, that night in the restaurant, I won't be able to decide what I want on the menu; everyone waiting and eventually I'll hand it to my friend, who sits next to me, asking her to choose for me.

She'll ask the waiter to get me some rice and some chamomile tea, and I'll say thank you. My spirit leaning wearily on hers.

And this, the goodness. This, the cut blossom blooming.

That night after packing, I check my email, find a baby update in my spam folder. I'd forgotten to cancel the updates. The email says *Congratulations, you are forty weeks and due any day to give birth.*

My water breaks all over the office floor, a deep pool of sorrow, leaving me emptied, gutted, wrecked.

Much like labor—without the child.

25

Out of Africa

Here I am, where I am supposed to be.

Isak Dinesen

January 2014

There are flash rains here, even in the dry seasons, pooling on the red dirt of Ugandan roads. There are black goats on the side of the road and children rolling tire tubes down the roads with sticks and kicking discarded Coke bottles like they're soccer balls.

Storks perched on traffic poles and roofs, and African violets singing purple from the trees.

Lake Victoria sits in the middle of everything—like a blue ribbon tying the country together. Families lie on its banks Saturday afternoons on blankets, others in boats fishing.

Hundreds of houses, nailed-together pieces of tin and plywood, a few mansions dotting the overlooking hills, and stores, all brightly colored with advertisements for teeth whitener and cell phone plans. Traffic is horns and motorcycles with families and babies, and stop signs ignored.

The sun is hot on the shaved and braided heads of the orphans we're holding. Their skin smells like bananas.

I am feeding a baby some plantain, mushed up with boiled potatoes and rice with a cream sauce. Grilled chicken in a paper bag and French fries for the foreigners, and we are at Destiny—a home for abandoned children found in the slums of Katwe and in the pediatric wing of the hospital.

Destiny is one of the schools funded by World Help.

This little girl was found, abandoned, in Katwe, and she has no aunties or uncles to buy her presents on her birthday, no daddy to swing her high in the air, no mommy to kiss her forehead and tuck her into bed at night. No one.

She's one year old. She wears a diaper and her brown eyes search mine silently as I spoon the plantain into her mouth, and she has slivers of wood through the lobes of her ears, tribal piercings—and I think about her mother, bearing her in the dirt of the slum, the smell of feces and fish outside their cloth door and the father—maybe he died of AIDS, maybe both of them did, and the grandmother starving to death, because life is not Facebooked here in Africa. It's not Instagrammed into edited photos. It's not a compilation of statuses, or cleverly worded tweets. No, life in the slums is about survival.

Around me are twenty others just like her—sitting quiet and still in their plastic chairs eating plates of food, and they don't complain once. So many cried so long with no response when they were babies that they learned not to cry. There is nothing sadder than a silent baby. It's a child who's given up hope.

I'm spooning plantain and potato and her small mouth moves, I give her some juice and her hair is tied up in colorful elastics. Her feet not touching the floor, and it's not fair.

This world we live in, this country with its 2.5 million orphans suffering for the sins of grown-ups—because of the sins of people like Joseph Kony—and it's the children who pay.

Her name is Kissa, and I hadn't seen her before today. We came here once before, and I carried another young girl on my hip—but she was older, with a long face.

Kissa has solemn brown eyes, a pouty bottom lip and tufts of brown hair.

I keep spooning plantain and potatoes until she lets out a tiny sigh. It's the first expression I've had from her, this quiet, polite sigh that tells me she's full, and I wipe her mouth with the edge of a napkin, hold out my arms.

Mama Josephine comes to the door, smiles at us foreigners on the floor, bowing before the children, serving them lunch, takes a seat—she lost her sister last month. Her husband, two years ago. She lives in a large home with twenty-five orphaned children; she runs Destiny, which cares for 1,700 more, and oversees a church in the slums which ministers to 2,500 each Sunday.

I hold Kissa gently. She's motionless except for a sniff from her nose, then she coughs. A friend of mine is asking Mama Josephine which babies are up for adoption, and she points to the girl in my arms, as well as a few others.

And there is my answer.

My womb has been closed only to open now. To hold children like Kissa. Because how can I try to make a daughter when so many little girls need a family?

"Please show me, Jesus," I'd prayed that morning, coming to Villages of Hope—that God would reveal to me if we were to adopt our daughter.

I wipe Kissa's nose with a napkin, and she is motionless, there in my arms.

I hold her on my hip for the next three hours and she plays with the pink ribbon around her waist, the front of her cotton dress stained. I change her diaper and she lies there quiet, as though she's used to being forgotten.

She fits in the crook of my arm and we sit together on the back porch of the rescue home, and I poke the bellies and tickle the feet of other children coming and going, but always, Kissa. And I softly trace the brown soles of her bare feet, and she looks up at me. Her eyes just staring at me like she's recognizing love for the first time, and it's not long before she's cooing. Gurgling and the sound startles me because she's been so quiet, and she reaches up with her hands, touches my face.

No one can tell me her story. No one knows anything except that she was abandoned and saved. No one knows her birthday or her last name, and yet here she is, on my hip. So very real and yet no record except for her breath on my hands.

"I love you," I say to Kissa's head, with its colorful elastics and tufts of hair, and I kiss her forehead.

The afternoon has passed and the team is packing up video gear and saying goodbye to the children with their new basketballs and jumping ropes and the children are clinging to our legs because there are only six housemothers—and not enough laps.

"Can I adopt her?" I say to Mama Josephine, pointing to Kissa. Mama nods. "Yes, sure."

And I believe it's that easy.

It's like losing my arm, this losing her, and I give her carefully to a housemother on the steps. Kissa doesn't look back at me, just sits on this new lap because she's used to being left.

And I walk to the bus, Uganda's red dirt on the soles of my feet and I think of Psalm 10, which a friend sent to me before I left.

> The victim's faint pulse picks up;
> > the hearts of the hopeless pump red blood
> > as you put your ear to their lips.
> Orphans get parents,
> > the homeless get homes. (vv. 17–18 Message)

I slam my fists on the steering wheel because I've forgotten my library card—it's in the other wallet and the kids are strapped into their car seats on our way to the library.

It's funny, how you can be both the best version of yourself and the worst version of yourself within the same week, across two entirely different continents.

I've been home for twenty-four hours and awake for thirty-six, with catnaps and fitful nights, and I swing the car around on the highway and Aiden begins to whimper in the backseat. I look in the rearview at my oldest son, who has my face. "What is it, Aiden?"

He won't tell me, just whines, and Kasher's pulling at his hood and asking me to take off his jacket and then I see that Aiden's lunch has fallen to the floor.

I speed home to get the missing card, clenching my jaw. There's no airplane bathroom to weep in, here. There's no complimentary glass of wine or time to journal, as there was on the plane heading back from five days in Uganda and Rwanda—five days of witnessing the effects of genocide and the Lord's Resistance Army, five days of holding orphans and seeing what God is doing in a world that wakes even as we sleep.

And then, home. Back to the land of white—white snow, white faces, and the white noise of first-world problems that no longer make me sympathetic. Including the complaints of my own sons.

I run into the house, grab the card. Trent calls, "You're back already?"

"I forgot my stupid card. Bye."

Back to the van, pick up Aiden's fallen lunch, slide into the front seat and then pause.

"Can we pray, boys?"

So we bow there, for a moment, and I ask God in a shaky voice to keep us safe and to give us good moments today, amen.

On the way home from Africa—the twenty-four-hour flight from Rwanda to Uganda, and then to Amsterdam, on to Seattle, and finally Edmonton, only to drive two hours to our tiny Dutch hamlet—my chest cavity was a hole. I'd never felt such an ache in my heart; I kept gasping in my seat, gasping for air because my chest would seize up for the pain.

It would only be relieved when I went to the tiny airplane bathroom and wept, hard. Sobbing for the people I'd left, for the pain I'd encountered and could not fix, for the faith I'd witnessed and the ripping of my body from Uganda's as I returned home—and then, the guilt.

The guilt of being so in love with a country when my family lives in another.

The pain in my chest—it was a new heart growing.

And the trick is, when God gives you a new heart, to ask him to make space for the old places and the old people who love you. Because it's not enough to just come home. It's not enough to enter the door and smell the wood smoke of a fire, to see the tiny boots of your sons and the larger ones of your husband, to hear Trent saying, "Mommy's home," and then the running of little feet and the boys taking the stairs and falling into your arms, your husband close behind. It's not enough.

Because you've been broken. Snapped in two for a world they do not know. You cannot bring back the smells—the smell of the sun on the heads of the children you did art with, the smell of boiled plantain and the dry sweat of the slums, the coffee with ginger. You can show them pictures. You can describe the storks standing tall on the traffic poles and the cows asleep in the middle of the traffic circle but you can't say too much or their eyes will glaze over.

But it helps, when Trent says he'd like to adopt Kissa too.

It helps bring Uganda closer to home, even as I fall against this farm boy with the strong arms.

"Yeah, I mean, I don't feel anything when I look at the picture," he says, pointing at the image of her in my arms. The boys in bed and us in the office talking—me on his lap, at his computer. "But if this is what God wants for our family, I'm fine with it. The feelings will follow."

"Can we pray about it?" I say.

"Of course." He takes my hands.

It's the only true posture our marriage knows, this one bowed low in prayer.

There's a book called *Follow Me* by David Platt, and in it he talks about his eldest son, whom he and his wife adopted from Kazakhstan. He writes,

> Adoption like this begins with a parent's initiative, not a child's idea. Before Caleb was even born in Kazakhstan, he had a mom and a dad working to adopt him. While Caleb was lying alone at night in an orphanage in Kazakhstan, he had a mom and a dad planning to adopt him. And one day when Caleb was placed in the arms of his mom and dad, he had no idea all that had been done, completely apart from any initiative in him, to bring him to that point. . . . This orphaned child became our cherished son because of a love that was entirely beyond his imagination and completely outside of his control.[1]

I picture our heavenly Father and all he did—all that he gave up—so that we could have a heavenly home.

When I think about Kissa found amid the rubble and trash of the slums, left skinny and dying by parents too starved to save her, when I think about how she had no one in the world besides Mama Josephine—who has hundreds of children and not enough beds—it doesn't matter the red tape, or the miles between us. It doesn't matter that it might take years.

It doesn't matter.

Because I see the way she reached up with her dimpled fingers and touched my face, the face of someone who'd held her for three hours and not grown tired of her, who'd changed her diaper and sung her "Jesus Loves Me" under Ugandan skies, who'd kissed away her tears and fed her plantain. The way she'd gurgled and cooed, like love was bubbling over, and "I won't forget, Kissa," I whisper.

1. David Platt, *Follow Me* (Carol Stream, IL: Tyndale, 2013), 28.

And then, the email.

The one from the adoption agency saying in cold font that Uganda is closed to international adoptions by Albertans.

I read and reread and supper is burning on the stove—sliced potatoes and carrots, sloppy-joe meat for buns, and the potatoes are black by the time I make it there, through a blur of tears.

Trent downstairs playing the Wii with Aiden and Kasher and *How can he be laughing?* I wonder. Now he's climbing the stairs, telling me something, and I'm pulling charred pieces of potato from the pan and he stops. "What's wrong?" he says at the top of the stairs.

Comes closer. I shake my head. "Albertans aren't allowed to adopt from Uganda."

"What?" He shakes his head. "Why not? Just Albertans?" He pulls me close. "It's okay, Em, it's going to be okay." It's the mantra of our marriage, him saying these words to me.

But my spirit cracks as he pulls me close, it cracks down the middle like a brittle bone. "She looks just like the girl in our dream . . ." I say into his shirt.

"I know. I know."

The Bible story that night after supper, around the table with the boys on our laps, is about Jesus turning loaves and fishes into food for multitudes, when there was near to nothing. No food except for a young boy's offering, and *It's all I have, Lord*, I tell him. *I just have this measly offering of faith—will you take it, and multiply it?*

Later that night I'm reading stories to Aiden and Kasher before bed and they choose one called *Wait and See*. It's by Robert Munsch, and it's all about this little girl who blows out her birthday candles and wishes for snow in summertime. "Wait and see," she says to people who don't believe it will happen, and I feel the Spirit whispering it to me too.

Wait and see, he says.

"God specializes in the impossible," my dad writes that night in an email.

I can see her now, running the hall in her bare feet, singing, the boys picking her up and tickling her—her smile splitting open, like the sun.

"Don't give up, Emily," Trent says as he walks out the door to play badminton, as he does every Monday night. "It's not over yet."

I nod and he turns, heads into the dark, closing the door behind him.

"Oh please, God," I say. "Don't let it be over yet."

26

Love

Define yourself radically as one beloved by God. This is the
true self. Every other identity is illusion.

Brennan Manning, *Abba's Child*

The next day I'm swollen and sore, like someone's burst my yellow balloon, and Kasher poops in his pants and I yell at him and
we both cry, there on the bathroom floor and Aiden comes, takes
my hand in his, his long face close to mine and you can smell the
sorrow: like seawater.

How can I adopt a daughter if I can't even take care of my
sons, I figure, and I sit on the couch and hold both of them, close,
tuck them under my arms like I'm trying to hide them back in my
womb and we read stories, but my heart is still in Africa, and I
hope it returns soon—on the next possible flight. My heart has
more stamps than my passport, it falls in love so fast.

"Do you always love this hard?" my teammate asked, our last
night in Kigali, Rwanda, at the long restaurant table. We'd spent

the day in the sun, in a white bus driving down bumpy red roads to the widow's village, children running alongside us and the founder of World Help asking the driver to stop the bus so the kids could get on.

I'd given away all our bottles of water at the widow's village, the women gathered around in a circle telling their stories and the staff filming it and holding babies, and the children by the bus begging for water. Their faces staring up at me, torn shirts and shoes with no laces. One boy saying, "Give me money."

I'd looked around, and none of the staff watching, I'd reached into the bus and grabbed the cardboard box full of unopened water bottles onto the dirt and the kids had mobbed it, crying and shoving, and I'd bitten the ends of my nails begging God that none of the staff would turn around.

And even in that moment I realized what a temporary fix this was, these few bottles of water. How these children needed the living water that rises from beneath our feet, a never-ending source.

When it was over and some of the children sore for not receiving a bottle, I walked slowly up to the photographer, said, "Um . . ."

He looked at me, this Canadian girl with the red kerchief around her neck. "You gave away all our water, didn't you?"

I looked down at the ground. "Yes."

He laughed.

A little while later, a woman named Margaret told me about her son and daughter, how they needed money for school because she'd just had an operation and I fumbled with my engagement ring, because the diamond seemed out of place. I thought about pawning it. Margaret's breath smelled of vodka, but she smiled so pretty in her bright print dress.

It's so hard to know when and how to give, but Margaret needed so much more than a ring—and the ring represented something so much more than money. It represented the man who'd committed himself to me, knelt down by a tree where he'd carved our initials, until death do us part.

"Yes, I always love this hard," I told him, sitting there, picking at the hotel food on my plate. All sectioned off and I wondered how many of the children I'd met that day would eat that night. Most Rwandans only eat one meal a day, if that.

To love—to have passion—means to suffer. It is the Passion of the Christ—the suffering of our Lord, and what is love if it isn't extravagant? If it isn't something that would die for someone else?

Truth is, I don't have much to boast about. Truth is, sometimes it's hardest to love those closest to you. I yell a lot and cry a lot and family looks like a lifetime of apologies.

Aiden's hair smells like oranges, here on the couch, and I kiss Kasher's soft round cheeks. "I love you boys—do you know that?"

Aiden nods.

"Yeah," says Kasher.

"And some kids don't have mommies or daddies," says Aiden. "We need to help them, right?"

"Yeah," says Kasher again. "And beds, and food, and wa-wa . . ."

I cup their faces.

I can't remember the day I didn't want to be a mother. The day I thought I could do life without one of these—one of these little bodies with their pants on backward and Diego underwear on their heads, mismatching socks and a spoonful of peanut butter in their hands. It's the hardest kind of love, this tearing open, but it's the making of heaven here on earth.

The boys are down for a nap and I sit at Trent's computer, in the chair I bought him off of Kijiji—wrapped in a red bow, the kind of chair that leans back—and I see that he's been browsing "Teaching English in Uganda." My heart leaps.

The phone rings. The Government of Alberta, call display reads, and they're returning my call: I'd left a long rambling message that morning about whether or not we could even consider adopting from Uganda as Canadians.

"It's not impossible—but it's very difficult," she says, and all I hear is, "It's not impossible."

I'm on the phone with Alberta's director of international adoption. "The Uganda government makes it very difficult, because they want to make sure their children are not being trafficked."

Her voice is quiet and smooth and I keep waiting for the hard part. And then it comes.

"You may have to move to Uganda for thirty-six months," she says. "I strongly encourage you to consider another country."

But how do you explain on the phone that she gurgled in your arms and touched your face, that she played with the ribbons on her dress and laughed in the African sun; how do you describe the smell of bananas on her skin, the stained front of her pink dress, the tiny feet that still hadn't learned how to walk?

"So it's not impossible?" I say.

The voice pauses. "No. It's not impossible."

That's all I need to hear.

We say goodbye and I lean my elbows on the desk and I don't know what this means.

Photos on the desktop of Danny and Sam and Oma and Opa, of smiles and laughter and Canada. There will always be needs, somewhere, and there will always be people without family, and I think again of her: of Leah, in the back of my van.

Of me asking her, in a corner booth in Wendy's over a container of chili and a cup of black coffee, "Do you have anyone I can take you to?" And this beautiful lady in an old man's jacket, who I'd found sleeping in the bathroom stall, shaking her head, and looking down.

"No," she'd said. "I have no one. No one in the world."

It's a sin for there to be orphans when there are so many people on this planet.

Everyone should have someone.

Everyone should have a family.

And this, why Jesus was born: to give each of God's sons and daughters a family that would never leave. That would never forsake. That would run down the path to meet them when they finally returned home.

"It's the greatest religion," I tell Trent that night.

"What is?" he says.

"Taking care of orphans and widows—it says, right here in James," and I read the Scripture on my laptop. "'Religion that God our Father accepts as pure and faultless is this: to look after orphans and widows in their distress,' chapter 1 verse 27."

The greatest religious act we can do is to be a family. Is to give someone a home. Perhaps it's not Kissa. Perhaps it is someone else. Perhaps this baby is only the beginning of God's dream.

I don't know if we'll be moving to Uganda for three years. The Alberta government may not even approve our wanting to adopt and then it's over, but there's still a chance. The door of heaven, cracked open, and I can see the light.

And the silhouette of a little girl, dancing.

I ache like the Grand Canyon; I know I've made the right decision because right often feels like dying, and yet there's a peace too. Kind of like a long run.

I haven't sent in the application. I haven't applied for international adoption, even after weeks of research and prayer and contacts, because the truth is—for the vast sum we are being asked to pay, with no guarantee of success—we can sponsor six children until they turn eighteen.

And local adoption is free. There are needy children everywhere. But Kissa still has no one.

"That must have been so hard for you," Trent says when he comes home from coaching basketball and I tell him I don't think it's wise to try to adopt Kissa. He pulls me close. "I'm fine with adopting local, as long as that's what you want," he says.

I don't know anymore. But I know what is right. I know true religion is taking care of orphans and widows.

Two nights later, after speaking with the local adoption agency and signing up for their training, I sob into the floor by the wood-stove. Ask God to speak to me about our daughter—the one missing from our family since the miscarriage last spring.

And then I go upstairs at midnight and choose five more children, in addition to the one we're already sponsoring, from Destiny Villages of Hope. And even as I send the email, requesting these children, I receive a message from a friend of mine whom I met in Korea years ago.

She had forwarded an old email of mine—the subject, "Birth Announcement," and it is the letter we'd sent out telling everyone about our eldest son's birth.

"I found this precious old email, Em," she said.

And in the first few lines of the forwarded message, I'd written,

"We celebrate, so very humbly, the birth of our beautiful babe: Aiden Grey. Our hearts are full. We have longed for a child, and God has heard our longing . . . may you be encouraged, in your own pursuits and dreams. He hears, and he is good."

It is enough. This random, very-much-planned coincidence is enough.

It is God saying, through my own words, *I heard your longing then, Emily, and I hear it now.*

27

The Lulu Tree

You might be poor, your shoes might be broken, but your mind is a palace.

Frank McCourt

February 2014

I'm kneeling on the carpet in front of the woodstove, praying into the wood chips and the spilled ash, like I do every night now when my family falls asleep.

It's been a month since I walked the slums in my pink shirt and blue jeans. The air smelled like despair there, like salt and soil, and I touched every hand possible, picked up every baby, because I couldn't hold Africa tightly enough.

It was a reunion for this girl who lived in the Congo and Nigeria for two years, my dad a missionary with Christian Blind Mission. In spite of the garbage in the streams, the barefooted babies with malnourished bellies, the aching fatigue of collapsing shacks, I was home.

And this has made coming back to Canada more than difficult. I was gone for only nine days—and yet it felt like a lifetime.

It's made me fall on my knees, night after night, for the memory of children without mothers or fathers, without food or water, without clothes. Children who had green snot running down their faces and no doctor to rush them to. I hurt over the lethargy and hopelessness of life in the slums—and yet there was Mama Josephine, rescuing babies, taking them with her to her orphanage and nursing them back to health.

Before I left on the bloggers' trip, God had said, *Your job is not to fix. I could fix the world with one breath. Your job is to love.*

But oh, with every ache of this mother's breath, I want to end the pain. I want to pack up and move to Uganda and give those babies a home, and it's been the hardest surrender.

Yet I know a Savior whose flag flies higher. I know a God who claims to do the impossible, and even as I fall on my face in my comfortable house in the snowy north of Alberta, Canada, I can see Jehovah rising furious over the slums of Africa and then gently placing down servants to bring about mercy.

Because when I walked those streets in Katwe, it wasn't me bending down to hold those children—it was God's love exploding through my skin. Desperate to let his people know he cares.

He sees those HIV-positive babies crying for mothers who won't come because they're dead. He sees those teenage boys sniffing glue to numb their hunger pangs. He sees those grandmothers working twenty-hour days to find enough food for their dead daughter's children who lie on the dirt floor while chickens defecate around them. And the four hundred families who lost everything in the fires that recently ripped through northern Uganda? Yeah, he sees them too.

And he weeps.

So I do too. And I know I'm not the only one to return from Africa and feel this way. But the question is: What am I going to do about it?

Because it's not enough to have a "changed perspective." That trip was not about me. It was about God inviting me into his heart—and his dreams—for Africa.

I pour myself a cup of coffee and glance at the women gathered in the fellowship hall of the church just a five-minute walk from our house.

The boys in Sunday school and nursery downstairs and I haven't been in weeks. The smell of perfume and coffee beans, babies in car seats at young mothers' feet and hymnbooks in our chairs. We'll sing a couple of songs and there's always a "share question," which makes us laugh awkwardly and talk about things like what we would be if we could be anything, or where we would go, and it wipes the dust off the covers of our lives—blows gently at the everyday and offering a glimpse at what lies beneath.

There's a girl with a yarn scarf wrapped around her neck and I haven't seen her before; I sit beside a friend and we talk about the week, small things, like the weather and our children growing faster than we can breathe, and then my friend nods toward the girl in the scarf sitting a few chairs away. "I love that—where did you buy it?" she says, pointing at the scarf.

The girl smiles. "I made it—it's so easy, it only takes twenty minutes!"

And immediately I think, *That's something I can teach Ugandan women to do.*

I'm not sure where the thought comes from, and I don't even know the girl's name, but I ask to talk with her before we disperse for our small groups.

She approaches me after the final song even as I'm leaving because I've forgotten. "About the scarf," she says, and I stop. "Oh yes! I was thinking—I just returned from Africa, and when you said you can make these in twenty minutes I thought these would be perfect for making with women in the slums."

Her eyes brighten. "I love that idea."

I laugh. Touch her arm. "What's your name, by the way?"

She smiles. "My name is Lysa. I'm new here."

And it's a beginning.

It's not everything, but it's something—like the faintest breeze and you can smell it, like spring, new upturned earth. It smells like Hope.

We spend a few days trying to think of a name for whatever it is we're doing, Lysa and I. And nothing is really right.

And then I spend a day in prayer. I play my guitar and I'm upturned on the carpet, pressed hard against the heart of God. And then I open my Bible and read about the pearl—the one for which the merchant sold everything in order to buy, because the kingdom of heaven is like one of these, Jesus says.

I know this too is something, because Uganda is called the pearl of Africa.

And as I'm driving the next day I think about the Pearl House—but this is already an organization in Africa. And then I think of the Pearl Tree. Jesus also likens the kingdom of God to a tree where birds flock to rest. And there's a whisper within me to find out what *pearl* is in Swahili, one of the national languages in Uganda.

It is Lulu.

The Lulu Tree.

I'm smiling and then typing in "the Lulu Tree" to see if it's already been taken, and what I find is that the Lulu tree is an actual tree in southern Africa.

It is a tree that grows shea nuts—called *lulu* in Arabic—and the tree itself lives up to three hundred years, with fifteen to twenty years of growth before fruiting. And this is what gets me—the tree's overwhelming bounty of nuts yields at the exact time of seasonal hunger, in addition to the nuts having extreme economic value.

This tree, it yields at the exact time of seasonal hunger.

I'm motionless.

I don't know much. I know we want to prevent tomorrow's orphans by equipping today's mothers, and the way to a mother's heart is through her children.

So we'll start with a pot of beans and a Bible.

We'll start by feeding the mothers.

And from there we meet, and befriend, and walk alongside them.

I'm reminded of visiting a training school in Gulu, Uganda, and slipping off even as the rest of the team dedicated schools. I walked to the nearby well where men and women were taking turns filling up their old yellow jugs. And I offered to help them. I struggled with the pump for a few minutes while they just stared. I laughed and sputtered along with the water, but for a minute it felt like we were one.

After that I wandered to the back of the school, found the cooks and dishwashers bent over fires and buckets of soapy water, making supper and washing dishes on the ground. I squatted beside one of them and began to wash. And even though we were squatting on the dirt, and their sponge was in tatters, the water was clean and they had a rinse bucket and a soapy bucket, and every dish sparkled.

They just giggled and handed me a fresh bucket of suds, a tattered cloth to wash with, and we worked side by side until I saw the rest of my group gathering to go.

We've come a long way, I know, and we're all trying our best, but I refused to Purell my hands on that trip. I refused to sanitize the kids' scent or the dust from my skin, because I want to feel what they feel. I want to live within their story and not just tell it. I want to touch the heart of Africa and not just take an edited photograph.

It's why Jesus was different from the other preachers and teachers. He not only spoke with authority he lived with authenticity. He refused to throw stones; he looked up and saw Zacchaeus in a tree and he didn't take a picture, he asked to come over for dinner. He partied with the sinners and before he healed the lepers he reached out and touched them. Because he knew it wasn't about saying nice words; it was about crossing that invisible line and touching humanity.

At one point on the trip we visited a school, and on the other side of the wire fence the unsponsored children with their mothers and fathers stood sadly, peering through at the children in their uniforms, and when I came close the mothers begged me to help their babies. Because education is the only thing dividing the poor from the rich.

And I reached across the wire and gave them a piece of paper and a pen to write down their names, so we could get them sponsored, and in the process I scratched my arm, a long, bloody mark.

It's about hurting for one another. It's about crossing the line and bleeding in the process. It's about kissing those snotty, dirty, beautiful children in the slums and walking down the garbage paths to shake hands with the men and hug the exhausted, skinny mothers. It's about crying over the dying babies in the hospital. It's about doing communion over a pot of beans underneath the heat of an African sun.

There is no me versus them. There is no missionary or unreached or developed country or developing.

There's only us.

And we all need the same thing.

We all need Jesus.

This, what I want for Lulu.

I want Jesus.

I want the lines to merge, and for us to lift one another up.

So we're searching for this pearl.

It's not the daughter I was dreaming of, this Lulu. But it's starting off so small and I'm tending to it like a mother, caring for it, nursing it, praying over it, begging God to help it grow.

Even as I fall on the floor every night among the wood shavings and remember her.

Africa.

28

Home

I believe the nicest and sweetest days are not those on which
anything very splendid or wonderful or exciting happens but
just those that bring simple little pleasures, following one
another softly, like pearls slipping off a string.

L. M. Montgomery

I'm making applesauce, pummeling the fruit with a pestle, and
Trent says, "I'm so proud of you."

I look at him, my hair sticking to my forehead. "This?" I say,
gesturing to the pile of skin and cores. "This makes you proud?"

He nods. "Aren't you proud of me when I make salsa or chop
wood?" he asks.

And I am, because there's something about physically sustaining your life. There's something about making home with your
hands, about feeding and clothing and cleaning and building in
a very practical way that allows you to feel grateful and quietly
awestruck.

And then there are days when we order Chinese takeout or cook a frozen pizza. When I just don't want to fold one more pile of laundry. When I scroll down my newsfeed on Facebook and feel like everyone's life looks more sparkly than mine. When I yell at my kids and then stub my toe. When I wish I could be anywhere but here and anyone but me.

But I have a Father who wants me to be here, who wants me to be me.

In February 2014, I stood in the Austin Music Hall in Texas, at a women's conference, the air dusky and more than a thousand women with their arms raised as though pushing away the darkness. My limbs ached from stretching but still I lifted them, as I had the previous spring in Nebraska, trying to touch my Abba.

The singer onstage with tattoo sleeves and a red beard spoke into the microphone, and he told us about his children. "I have four," he said, "and three—two boys and a girl—are adopted. I only have one daughter though, and I can tell you that while my love for all of my children, adopted and biological, is of equal value, the love I have for my daughter is distinct. Special. It's the same amount of love, but it's a different kind—and that's the way it is with Abba's love for his daughters. He has a special kind of love for you women."

We began to worship then, our voices rising into the darkness, our arms reaching high—the tables scattered with journals and books and pens and water bottles—and when the singer stopped and listened to us, you could hear a unified chorus of Abba's daughters—a tidal wave of harmony—for all of us being in unison, and the roof fairly split open and angels descended.

And even as I sang, my arms shaking, I remembered Madeleine, my baby with the angels; Kissa, my African daughter without a mother or father; Leah and Ashley, my Canadian sisters struggling to make it home. I cupped them all with my palms and pressed their prayers into the heart of a Father whose face was so close to earth I could smell his breath—like some kind of earthy incense.

He showed me a picture of myself, at eighteen, in Bible school, my long blonde hair and my bell-bottom jeans, and I was doing a belly laugh, one of those full-throated guffaws, and he said, "I love that girl."

And I felt the same way I did two months ago, when I was walking downstairs to go to bed. The house asleep, except for Trent reading beneath the feather tick in our bed, the walls quietly dozing and the fire in the woodstove crackling orange and red against the glass. I stepped off that last stair, raising a hand to tuck a piece of hair behind my ear, and I stepped right into love.

A full-throated, hearty kind of love, the kind that sweeps you up in the biggest embrace, the kind that sings over you while you sleep, and I knew, without a doubt, for the first time in my life that it was good to be Emily Theresa Wierenga. It was good to be me. In fact, heaven was applauding her—that little girl in the mushroom cut with the large plastic glasses and the pink sweatpants—it was twirling her and laughing with her and kissing her.

As heaven applauds all of its daughters—whether they're in the slum of Katwe, Uganda, or on the frostbitten streets of Edmonton, Alberta.

And not because of anything we've done. We can never do enough. But only because of the extraordinary love of an Abba who risks everything—who runs down that road, his cloak flapping in the wind—to meet his prodigals.

And when I get tempted to forget what matters?

That's when I pull my boys close. I get down on the floor and embrace this quiet, humble, serving life. The kind that becomes bigger the smaller you get.

Life around the coffee table—the one made of boards from Papa Wierenga's homemade sawmill, thirty-five years ago.

Our life. It may not be glamorous, but it's ours. With all of its tears and peanut butter smudges, with all of its wine stains on the carpet and laundry heaped high.

And we're making it home.

Epilogue

September 2014

"The heartbeat is fast—166 beats per minute," the technician told me in the blue hush of the ultrasound room.

"Is that good?" I said.

"Oh yes, that's very good—very strong."

Then he told me to hold my breath and I did, and then released as he played back the sound he'd just recorded—the beautiful "ba-boom, ba-boom" of life, its fluid line sketched across the screen and the baby's arms and legs kicking like tiny sticks on a peanut.

Our child was two centimeters—just over an inch, at nine weeks, two days old.

"It's implanted perfectly—it's got a beautiful place in your uterus. It's very comfortable," he said, smiling at me, knowing this was my fifth pregnancy but only the third to make it this far.

And finally I let myself smile back.

My baby was comfortable.

My body was making a home for this little one, and the insides of my soul relaxed. And for a moment it felt like the past year and

215

a half of trying for, and then conceiving and miscarrying and then grieving and trying again—it was all worth it.

Because after losing a couple of babies, you learn—even as you take folic acid and prenatal pills and progesterone to protect the conception—you learn also to protect your heart.

Trent was sitting with me on the bed in the dimly lit room, our baby dancing on the screen. He looked over and his fingers played with mine. And it didn't just feel like another baby—who was alive and comfortable and growing well. It felt like God saying, *See how I keep my promises—even when they look different than you expected?*

That day in the ultrasound room, our peanut swishing across the screen to the *thump, thump, thump* of life—like horses galloping— I felt hope rise within me.

And on March 11, 2015, at 12:44 a.m., we held to our hearts a beautiful girl—a daughter, Aria Hope, borne of his faithfulness.

It may not make sense right now.

Your faith might feel like that abandoned building.

But God does not play tricks on us. You can trust him. He does allow us to walk through fires and floods and earthquakes and famines, yes, but he is right there with us, going through all of it at our side, because he cares.

He will never leave you nor forsake you. He delights in you, sings over you, and desires to quiet you with his love.

And we can say with confidence—we, a throng of women on bended knee—"I will see the goodness of the Lord in the land of the living" (Ps. 27:13).

Acknowledgments

Writing a book is never a solitary process. It's lonely, yes, but only because one is surrounded by so many intangible characters who become much like a family, and you long to reach through the pages and touch them. To somehow be forgiven by them.

And only more so with memoir. Because the people you write about *are* family.

And they have given you pieces of their hearts in letting you write their stories. They have allowed you to enter their living rooms, sacred and hallowed places, and more than that they've given permission for you to share those living rooms—with all of their stained carpets and crooked picture frames—with the world. I want to thank these brave souls.

My Dad, whose servant-heart is a tireless reminder of Christ; my Mum, who has drawn close to heaven's doors due to cancer's return; my siblings, Keith, Allison, and Meredith, who've become dear friends; and my Nanny, whose passing I still grieve. I'm so grateful for your patience with me as I've written my way to healing. You've shown me the grace of God.

My father-in-law, Harvey, my mother-in-law, Marge, and my sisters-in-law, Teneale and Teshah, as well as Grandma Wierenga and Grandma Neumann: thank you for letting me sit with you at the farm table and for welcoming me into your conversations and hearts.

Ashley, whom I hold as a sister, her sons Danny and Sam, and Leah—the woman in the man's coat who has nowhere to call home. You are the bravest of the brave.

My mentor, Michelle, who invited me to Portland and then into Abba's throne-room. Without you I'd still be a nomad.

My Baker family—you've believed in me since the beginning. Thanks to Chad Allen, for nurturing my stories: without you, my words would be barren. Ruth Anderson, Erin Bartels, Lauren Carlson, Brianna DeWitt, Mark Rice, Lindsey Spoolstra, and the rest of the Baker team: your tireless efforts put my stories onto bookshelves. I am so grateful.

My agent, Chip MacGregor, who cheered me on from the sidelines—your integrity and prayers are such a gift.

Trenton—my life would be a blank page without you. You are my color, my song, the one who makes me laugh and who holds me when I cry. I can't imagine doing any of this without you. My dear sons, Aiden Grey and Kasher Jude—you inspire me daily, with your tender hearts, your sticky kisses and your big hugs. I am so honored to be your mother. And precious Aria Hope—how we've waited for you, beautiful daughter. Your life is an answer to prayer.

And finally, my Savior, Jesus Christ, without whom I am dust. You are the Word, and the only Book worth reading. Thank you for making your home in me.

Even as I make my way home.

Proceeds from this book will benefit The Lulu Tree (www.the lulutree.com), a charitable organization established by this author to prevent tomorrow's orphans by equipping today's mothers in the slums of Katwe, Uganda.

Emily T. Wierenga is an award-winning journalist, columnist, artist, author, blogger, and founder of The Lulu Tree. Her work has appeared in many publications, including *Christianity Today*, *The Better Mom*, *A Deeper Story*, *The Gospel Coalition*, *Desiring God*, *Adbusters*, *Geez Magazine*, *MOPS*, Dayspring's *(in)courage*, and *Focus on the Family*. She speaks regularly about her journey to freedom from anorexia, and makes her home in Alberta, Canada, with her husband, Trenton, and their three children. For more info, please visit her online at www.emilywierenga.com.

Also Available from Emily . . .

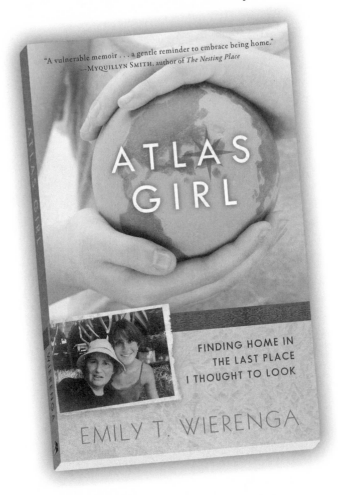

"A vulnerable memoir . . . a gentle reminder to embrace being home."
—Myquillyn Smith, author of *The Nesting Place*

ATLAS GIRL

FINDING HOME IN
THE LAST PLACE
I THOUGHT TO LOOK

EMILY T. WIERENGA

"Emily shares the unexpected beauty God had
created in her broken places and how he
can do the same for you."

—**Holley Gerth**, bestselling author of
You're Already Amazing

CATCH UP WITH
ARTIST, AUTHOR, AND
EVERYDAY RADICAL

emily
wierenga

ON HER BLOG AT
EMILYWIERENGA.COM

 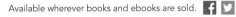